Advocates in Action

Making a Difference for Young Children

Adele Robinson and Deborah R. Stark

An NAEYC Comprehensive Membership Benefit

National Association for the Education of Young Children
Washington, D.C.

Photographs copyright © by
CLEO Photography: 19
Mary K. Gallagher: 110
Bill Geiger: back cover—bottom
Jean-Claude LeJeune: cover—middle, 64, 92
Jonathan Meyers: 42, back cover—middle
Marilyn Nolt: cover— top right & bottom
Daniel Raskin: cover—top left, back cover—top
Subjects & Predicates: 7

National Association for the Education of Young Children
1509 16th Street, NW
Washington, DC 20036-1426
202-232-8777 or 800-424-2460
www.naeyc.org

Through its publications program the National Association for the Education of Young Children (NAEYC) provides a forum for discussion of major
issues and ideas in the early childhood field, with the hope of provoking
thought and promoting professional growth. The views expressed or
implied are not necessarily those of the Association. NAEYC thanks the
authors, who donated much time and effort to develop this book as a
contribution to the profession.

Library of Congress Control Number: 2001098593
ISBN 1-928896-01-4
NAEYC #117

Publications editor: Carol Copple
Managing editor: Natalie Cavanagh
Copyediting: Brian Baker and Sandi Collins
Editorial assistance: Lacy Thompson
Design and production: Malini Dominey

Printed in the United States of America

About the authors

Adele Robinson is the Director of Public Policy and Communications for NAEYC, overseeing federal and state policy and public communications. She has worked on the reauthorization of the Elementary and Secondary Education Act, the Higher Education Act, the Child Care and Development Block Grant, annual federal appropriations bills, and many others. Prior to joining NAEYC, Ms. Robinson was a Senior Program Associate in the Government Relations division of the National Education Association and was Director of Government Relations for the National Association of State Boards of Education. She was a Legislative Assistant to the U.S. Senate Committee on Labor and Human Resources, responsible for legislation relating to early childhood, elementary and secondary education, and higher education. In addition, she has written model legislation for states in the areas of teacher quality, charter schools, and reading instruction. She received her B.A. from Yale University and her J.D. from Boston University School of Law.

Deborah Roderick Stark is a consultant with broad experience in child and family policy and programs. As Special Assistant to the Commissioner of the Administration on Children, Youth and Families of the U.S. Department of Health and Human Services during the Clinton Administration, she designed and implemented Congress' 1993 Family Preservation and Support initiative and the 1994 Early Head Start program. Prior to this, she was a policy analyst for the bipartisan National Commission on Children. She also worked in the San Francisco Bay Area designing new community programs for children and families. Her publications include the *Collaboration Basics* series (1999) and the education and child welfare chapters in *Beyond Rhetoric: A New American Agenda for Children and Families* (1991). She received her B.A. from Wellesley College and her M.S.W. from the University of California at Berkeley. Deborah is the mother of three young children and divides her time between Maryland and California.

Acknowledgments

The authors are very grateful for the insights of the following people who shared their experiences as advocates and as trainers of advocates:

Lereen Castellano, Family Star; Shirley Craighead; Christy Dees, Texas Interagency Council on Early Childhood Intervention; Melinda Felice, Parent Voices; Elaine Fersh, past director of Parents United for Child Care; Carol Fichter, Nebraska Early Childhood Training Center; Jon Gould, Children's Alliance; Chad Griffin, former campaign manager for Proposition 10 and "No on Proposition 28"; Jack Lightfoot, Child and Family Services of New Hampshire; Sessy Nyman, Day Care Action Council; Karen Ponder, Smart Start; Judy Reidt-Parker, People's Regional Opportunity Program; Sue Russell, Child Care Services Association of North Carolina; Geelea Seaford, Smart Start; Judy Victor, Day Care Justice Co-op, Inc.; Sharon Walsh, Division for Early Childhood of the Council for Exceptional Children; and Patti Wooley, Child and Family Services, Kennebec Valley Community Action Program.

In addition, we would like to thank Helen Blank of the Children's Defense Fund, Ron Cowell of the Education Leaders Policy Center, Mary Babula of the Wisconsin Early Childhood Association, and Joan Lombardi of Better Baby Care for their reviews of earlier drafts.

Barbara Willer, Carol Copple, Sandi Collins, and Natalie Cavanagh of the National Association for the Education of Young Children advised us as we worked on the project.

Finally we would like to especially thank Stacie Goffin and Joan Lombardi for blazing the trail for this publication by authoring *Speaking Out: Early Childhood Advocacy*. We hope this book will provide motivation and support to lead advocates into a new era of advocacy, as did its predecessor.

This book is dedicated to Helen Hollingshed Taylor whose life and career epitomized the ideals of an advocate in action. She was unwavering in her vision for excellence in early childhood education for every child, every family, and every professional. Everything that Helen did supported this vision—setting high standards for children and staff, providing support to achieve the standards, and fostering partnerships between programs, families, and communities. Because of her work, millions of children and families have gained access to better early childhood experiences and the early childhood profession has grown in stature.

Contents

Preface

In 1988 NAEYC published *Speaking Out: Early Childhood Advocacy* by Stacie Goffin and Joan Lombardi. The authors and NAEYC sought to inspire and encourage early childhood professionals and the public to advocate on behalf of young children. Many gains have been made as a result of the collective efforts of early childhood advocates. For example, more than 40 states fund prekindergarten programs for four-year-olds, although only one state makes these programs universally available. Several states have a stipend or bonus for early childhood program staff tied to increased professional development, and many states provide a higher reimbursement rate for child care programs meeting higher standards or that have been accredited. Advocates have encouraged legislatures and other policymakers to use funds from lotteries, dedicated tax streams, and other financing mechanisms to help make early childhood education more affordable and of higher quality.

At the federal level, infants and toddlers can benefit from Early Head Start, and families have help with child care costs under the Child Care and Development Block Grant. For children in the primary grades, there are more opportunities for after-school programs through the 21st Century Community Learning Centers, for their teachers to have preparation and ongoing professional training in research-based reading instruction, and their schools to receive grants to help connect to new technologies. And, more than ever, business and community leaders are joining in by speaking out for children and high quality programs at all levels—local, state, and national.

Yet there is still much to accomplish. Far too many children live in poverty. Their families have limited access to high-quality early childhood programs. Many neighborhood school buildings are overcrowded and lack classroom computers and a well-stocked library. Family leave is out of reach for many parents. Advocates will need to be even more creative, strategic, and collaborative to ensure that all children have access to high-quality early childhood education.

It is NAEYC's hope and goal that this new book, building on the tradition of *Speaking Out*, will help early childhood advocates, particularly in the arena of federal and state public policy. The book provides more detailed information on public policy by nonprofit organizations using paid and volunteer advocates, the use of technology with grassroots networks, media and public communication, and the federal and state legislative processes. This book also shares examples of "Advocates in Action," profiles of exciting real life advocacy efforts and the lessons learned from them.

Acting together, we can fulfill one of NAEYC's goals—to improve public understanding and support and funding of high-quality programs. Centers, homes, and schools serving young children and their families can benfit from public policy initiatives and public awareness and engagement activities. It will take all of us to make this happen.

Acting together, we can make a difference for young children, their families, and our profession.

—*Kathy R. Thornburg*
President, NAEYC

Why is Advocacy Important?

Today's babies and young children will be tomorrow's parents, doctors, entrepreneurs, teachers, and religious and civic leaders. But do we as a country care enough about our children and their well-being to invest in them during their early years? More often than not, there is a lot of *rhetoric* about the importance of children but little *action* to match that rhetoric.

As a nation of great wealth, many of our children and families are not yet sharing in the prosperity:

❖ more than one in six children under age 18 live in poverty;[1]

❖ more than 50 percent of children under age six who live in a single-mother household are poor;[2]

❖ ten million children have no health insurance;[3]

❖ our child care providers are among the lowest earners among all workers, with an average salary of just $15,430 per year;[4] and

❖ nearly 25,000 public school buildings are dilapidated, overcrowded, and cannot be connected to new technologies.[5]

In part, this failure to invest sufficiently in the health and cognitive, social, and emotional development of our youngest children is due to a lack of understanding among policymakers and the public of the importance of the early years. Only recently has the latest research on the impact of early development and learning been translated by researchers or advocates in a way that speaks directly to policymakers and stimulates them to action.

Children are cared for by their families as well as by the staff and administrators of early childhood education programs—both need assistance in the research-based practices that support all children's development and learning. In fact, 59 percent of women with infants under the age of one were in the labor force in 1998, and 73 percent of mothers with children one year or older were employed, with 52 percent working full-time.[6] And for much of the year, children in school rely on teachers and other staff to help them learn to high academic standards and to be respectful of others.

We can allow policies and funding to remain as they are, or we can work together with other families, neighbors, coworkers, organizations, and policy leaders on a common vision and set of goals. This is why advocacy is important.

Here are some indicators of where we are and where we need to go to realize real investment and support for all families and all children:

Look at federal policies, programs, and budget decisions. Are the investments in our children's and families' health, education, and economic stability equal to the needs? Although the federal government spends more than $10 billion annually on child care assistance and Head Start, the number of children without access to high-quality early childhood education remains significant. Although roughly $9 billion dollars is spent on Title I schools to help students reach academic standards, many schools and students still lack resources that would level the playing field with schools in more affluent communities.

❖ A recent report by the U.S. Department of Health and Human Services shows that only 12 percent of the children eligible under the Child Care and Development Block Grant receive assistance.[7]

❖ The current funding level for Head Start serves only 3 in 5 of the eligible children and many programs are less than full-day and full-year.[8]

❖ Congress agreed to fund 40 percent of the cost of special education and related services under the Individuals with Disabilities Education Act, but current funds are far below that goal; and

❖ The Family and Medical Leave Act requires employers to provide leave for up to 12 weeks, but applies only to employers with 50 or more employees and does not require employees to be paid during their leave.

Look at state policies, programs, and budgets. States spend even less, in aggregate, on early childhood education than the federal government does. Although states spend much more on elementary and secondary school education than the federal government, their own courts have pronounced distribution of school funds unconstitutional because the unequal amount of funds given to different districts promotes inequality of education. The following questions need to be answered: What portion of state budgets is devoted to early childhood care and education? What are states doing to ensure access to the quality, affordable care that all children need and deserve? What are states doing to ensure that children have qualified teachers, up-to-date textbooks, healthy and safe buildings, and other support for learning?

Sadly, some of the answers are as follows:

❖ In total child development and family support spending in 2000, six states invested more than $200 per child under age six, while 14 states spent $20 or less.[9]

❖ Although nearly two-thirds of states now fund at least one program that targets infants and toddlers and at least one aimed at preschoolers, five states (Alabama, Mississippi, South Dakota, Utah, and Wyoming) fund no child development or family support programs for young children and families.[10]

❖ Almost all of the states have been sued for failing to equitably and adequately finance public elementary and secondary education under each state's respective constitution, and nearly half have had to revise their school funding formula and other mechanisms to help children in low income school districts.

Look at the private sector. What are businesses doing to support the child care needs of their workers? What are businesses doing within their neighborhoods and states to support child care and early education so that their future employees get a good start?

One study found that only nine percent of the companies surveyed offered child care at or near the work site, only five percent offered child care vouchers to employees, and only nine percent financially supported local child care efforts.[11] Instead, companies were more likely to provide employees with information about child care availability in their community (36 percent) and offer plans that assist employees in paying for child care with pretax dollars (50 percent of companies with 100 or more employees).[12]

Advocates in Action: Making a Difference for Young Children provides practical guidance to concerned individuals and the early childhood community about advocacy on behalf of children. The authors recognize that advocacy takes place at many different levels—from families who approach their child's teacher or program director to ask for an arts program, to teachers who approach the school board to request additional funding for books to help their students meet rigorous academic standards, to groups of business leaders who form coalitions with early childhood caregivers, to professional associations who create opportunities to educate policymakers about a particular problem that young children face. At all these levels of advocacy, caring adults take a stand on behalf of children.

Chapter 1 summarizes different kinds of advocacy and stresses that our roles as advocates can be as intensive or informal as we desire. We each must decide what level of advocacy feels best.

Regardless of your previous experience (or inexperience) as an advocate or the level at which you have participated, you can find some reassuring advice in Chapter 2. Chapter 2 outlines key components of effective advocacy to consider, such as:

❖ getting organized

❖ creating a proactive agenda

❖ developing the message

❖ working with others

After absorbing the basic principles, advocates can become more proactive in the ways they use the legislative and regulatory processes to influence policy outcomes. Chapter 3 (along with materials in the appendix) provides essential information about how the federal and state legislative and regulatory processes work, and Chapter 4 gives insight into other policy opportunities with boards and commissions, ballot initiatives and referenda, and the judicial branch.

Chapter 5 offers a toolbox of ideas for influencing political systems—from organizing e-mail and phone trees, to conducting personal visits, to giving testimony and formulating language for legislation.

Using the media to raise public awareness about a problem and build momentum for your agenda can be highly beneficial. Chapter 6 presents tips for determining whether your issue is newsworthy and for preparing your approach to the media. The chapter also suggests exciting public-engagement activities that can help increase awareness of early childhood issues.

Chapter 7 gives information about voter education and political activity. Many organizations erroneously assume they cannot lobby or participate in the political arena. The chapter gives some introductory lessons on what nonprofits can and cannot do.

Sprinkled throughout the book are examples of "Advocates in Action"—profiles of exciting advocacy work from all over the country that elevate awareness and attention to early care and education issues. From a community in Denver, Colorado, that drove out drug dealers and turned a crack house into a Montessori infant and toddler center, to a "virtual strike" in New Hampshire, advocates are joining forces to call for changes that benefit young children in their communities.

Until all children in America have access to high-quality, developmentally appropriate early childhood and early grade experiences, and until all early childhood providers and teachers are able to receive the training and financial support they require to keep them in the field and ensure their commitment and competence, as many advocates as possible are needed to speak out on behalf of children. This means that families, early childhood providers, teachers and administrators have a dual role to play: First, they must be the principle nurturers of young children, giving them the stimulation, environments, and experiences they need to thrive. Second, they must translate their knowledge and strong commitment into advocacy, working to ensure that the policies, practices, and investments made by our schools, governments, and businesses are right for our children.

Endnotes

1. J. Dalaker, & B.D. Proctor, *Poverty in the United States*, U.S. Bureau of the Census, Current Population Reports, Series P60–210 (Washington, DC: U.S. Government Printing Office, 1999).
2. *Ibid.*
3. U.S. Census Bureau, *Health insurance detailed table: 1999*, Current Population Survey (Washington, DC: U.S. Government Printing Office, 2000).
4. Children's Defense Fund, *The state of America's children yearbook, 2001* (Washington, DC: Author, 2001), 46.
5. American Institute of Architects, *Talking points: School construction and modernization* (Washington, DC: Author, 2000).
6. U.S. Census Bureau, "Record share of new mothers in labor force, Census Bureau reports," *United States Department of Commerce News* (24 October 2000).
7. U.S. Department of Health and Human Services, *National Study of Child Care for Low-Income Families*, State and Community Subsidy (Washington, DC: U.S. Government Printing Office, 2000).
8. Children's Defense Fund. *Every child deserves a head start* (Washington, DC: Author, 2001). Available online: http://www.childrendefense.org/cc_facts.htm. Accessed November 14, 2001.
9. N.K. Cauthen, J. Knitzer, & C.H. Ripple, *Map and track state initiatives for young children and families* (New York: National Center for Children in Poverty, 2000).
10. *Ibid.*
11. E. Galinsky, & J.T. Bond, *The 1998 Business Work-Life Study: A sourcebook* (New York: Families and Work Institute, 1998).
12. *Ibid.*

CHAPTER 1

The Different Kinds
of Advocacy

S ome early childhood activists can't wait to meet with legislators,
giving data and research about child care policies and pushing for a
commitment to children and their families. Some parents are itching to
talk to their employer about expanding the company's family-friendly
policies to include more time off for them to do things with their kids.
Some teachers feel compelled to talk with their friends and neighbors
about the well-being of young children while they are in line at the
store, playing with their children at the park, or attending a community
event. All three of these examples represent advocacy. All kinds of
advocacy are important in the quest to improve the lives of children and
their families.

There are different forms of advocacy: personal advocacy, public policy
advocacy, and private-sector advocacy. Depending on your level of comfort
speaking out or reaching out, your desire to tackle an issue, your passion,
and your time and energy, you can decide how you can make a difference
in early care and education. As you feel more comfortable speaking out,
you can join with others to bring together all these forms to make a difference for children, families, and communities. Of course, the more people
who are a part of an intentional advocacy effort, the stronger the collective
voice and the more likely that change will be brought about as a result of
the advocacy efforts.

From Crack House to Early Childhood Center—

In the late 1980s a group of parents in a mostly Latino neighborhood in Denver, Colorado, grew frustrated by increased gun violence and drug trafficking in their community and took action into their hands. With the support of the principal from the Montessori magnet elementary school that was located across the street from a crack house, the parents organized themselves, community activists, and political leaders to take back the house. They cleaned up the outside of the house; found out who the owner was; raised funds from a local law firm, United Way, and several local foundations; and bought the house. In doing this, they sent a message to the drug traffickers that they wanted a safe neighborhood and a peaceful community for their children.

A community meeting was called about what to do with the house. Parents suggested that it should be made into a child care center because they were concerned that their children were entering school at a disadvantage and they wanted to begin from birth to help children reach their fullest potential. They wanted the center to be integrated culturally, racially, and economically, as was the public Montessori elementary school. Neighbors were recruited to participate in an intense Montessori teacher training. On January 14, 1991, the doors to one infant classroom and two toddler classrooms opened.

Family Star became one of the first Early Head Start programs when it received funding in 1995, and it is one of 17 research sites for the Early Head Start national evaluation. In 1998, Family Star was honored at the White House as an example of a program that makes a difference in the lives of Latino youth.

Accomplishments

Family Star met with the following successes:

• *involving parents.* Parents led the effort to take back the crack house and turn it into the infant and toddler center. But the involvement of parents didn't end there. Today the

Parents in Denver Transform their Community

program has very high parent involvement, with 75 to 85 percent of parents turning out for center meetings and related events. The strong relationships between parents and staff make it possible for the program to identify and address various needs of families (e.g., mental health issues, counseling, substance abuse, violence, parenting support) beyond providing quality child development experiences for the children.

• building support from beyond the immediate neighborhood. The families who sent their children to the public Montessori magnet school came from several neighborhoods throughout Denver. Even though their children were bused to the school, the parents joined with the local community to take back the crack house. They cared about the community and eagerly joined forces with the local neighbors to make the community a safe, beautiful place to live in and raise children.

• helping people understand that the impossible can be possible. Family Star was able to confirm people's beliefs that their neighborhood could and should be safe, that the Montessori education model could and should be available for infants and toddlers, and that the Montessori approach could and should be offered to diverse populations of children.

• supporting and nurturing staff. Very close attention has been given to developing staff from the local community and supporting them so they can provide high-quality care to the children. Identifying how best to support staff and their needs has been important to the success of the program.

Lessons learned

• Always let your principles be your guide.
• Be persistent.
• Know you can change the world for families and their babies.

Based on a telephone interview in January 2001 with Lereen Castellano, executive director of Family Star.

Personal advocacy

Personal advocacy is about sharing our personal views and philosophies with other individuals and groups. It is generally informal and spontaneous in nature, but it can be purposeful and well planned. With personal advocacy, the advocate raises awareness about an issue. Here are two examples of personal advocacy.

❖ Maria was concerned about the safety of the neighborhood playground. While pushing her toddler on the swing, she mentioned to the mother next to her that she was frustrated by the litter in the park, including the broken glass in the sandbox. The two women agreed to ask other parents and neighbors to come back the next day with trash bags and gloves to pick up litter while taking turns playing with the children.

❖ Juan organized early childhood care providers in his neighborhood to speak out about the need for more early care and education courses at the community college. The group wanted the courses to be offered in the evenings or on weekends so that more providers could participate. Juan sent a letter signed by all the providers asking the president and board of directors of the college to address the issue at its next meeting. He followed up with calls to ensure that the group's issue would be on the agenda. At the board meeting, Juan and his colleagues presented the issue, indicated how many providers in the community would take additional classes if they were offered at convenient times, shared their research on the link between training and quality care, and offered a motion that the board establish a committee consisting of local child care providers and college representatives to plan an expanded curriculum and a schedule that would suit the continuing-education needs of providers.

Public policy advocacy

Public policy advocacy, the primary focus of this book, is about influencing public policies and practices so that they are more responsive to issues affecting a large number of children. That means that public policy advocates challenge school boards and local, state, and federal policymakers and agencies by calling attention to problems and proposing solutions. Advocates demand that the stewards of public funds develop laws, regulations, and program guidelines that support early childhood education in appropriate ways. Two examples of such advocacy are as follows:

❖ A coalition of national organizations representing child care, schools, community agencies, and faith-based institutions focused on increasing funds for child care assistance and Head Start. The coalition decides to meet regularly to develop strategies, send joint letters to policymakers, and visit Congress. These efforts are supported by calls made to Congress by the coalition's grassroots networks.

❖ Members of the local child care planning council were frustrated with changes the state legislature was contemplating in the allocation of preschool funds. The council agreed to send a letter to state legislators as well as to those policymakers who chair the appropriate committees in the legislature. When a hearing was called on the issue, the planning council sent a representative to offer testimony about how the potential change would affect the local community and about how proposed alternatives would be most beneficial to providers and children.

Private-sector advocacy

Private-sector advocacy is about changing private-sector policies and practices to support children and families. Private-sector advocates educate business leaders about the need to implement family-friendly work policies and to invest in early childhood programs, schools, and after-school programs in their community and state to ensure that workers have quality child care options for their children. Private-sector advocates also challenge manufacturers of children's toys, computer games, and videos and the entertainment industry in general to make sure that children are not exposed to unnecessary violence. Many times, private-sector advocacy develops into advocates bringing business leaders into coalitions working to change public policies such as universal preschool or child health insurance. The following examples are illustrative:

❖ A shortage of space, a shortage of providers, and low wages were primary concerns in a community where most parents worked full-time jobs. Recognizing the need to develop new facilities and rebuild old ones, child care providers worked with a local bank to set up a fund that would give providers low-interest loans for facilities. At the same time, providers began to survey local businesses to see what investments they were making in child care for their employees. Only a few innovative employers were providing financial support to their employees with young children. The child care providers organized a breakfast briefing for employers to hear the latest statistics on the need for and availability of child care and to learn about data on quality child care and worker productivity. The child care community outlined how the employers could help address the local child care crisis and, at the same time, meet an increasingly urgent need of their own employees.

❖ A group of teachers and principals, joined by parents, approached local businesses about the lack of technology capacity in local schools. They talked to the businesses about the use of educational technologies to help children learn and become

---

Actions Early Childhood Advocates Can Take

You can choose from many courses of action once you make a commitment to become an advocate for children, their communities, and the early childhood profession. Here are a few choices:

• Share research that supports effective and appropriate practice with teachers and parents.

• Join an organization's public policy committee or agree to respond to a legislative telephone or e-mail tree.

• Write to the editor of a newspaper or magazine to respond to an article or letter.

• Talk with an employer about the needs of working parents, and ask for specific family-friendly policies such as telecommuting, job sharing, time off to attend doctors' appointments and special school events for your child, and other policies that help parents balance work and family requirements.

• Volunteer to join your professional group's advocacy committee to help plan and grow how the group will speak out on the health, social, and educational needs of young children.

• Collect data and research and develop with others a position statement on a critical issue.

• Volunteer to speak at a school board meeting about an NAEYC position statement and explain why the school board should adopt a certain policy.

• Conduct a local or state survey of salaries in early childhood programs.

Adapted by permission from S. Goffin & J. Lombardi, *Speaking Out: Early Childhood Advocacy* (Washington, DC: NAEYC 1988), 14–15.

---

computer-literate for the workplace demands of the twenty-first century. As a result, businesses agreed to volunteer time and resources to connect the schools to the Internet and to help set up computers in the classrooms. The businesses also volunteered a certain amount of technical assistance to schools in using new hardware and software. Both the local children and businesses benefited as a result. Children and teachers were able to use the latest tools for teaching and learning, and local businesses had enhanced their status as community members.

❖ Appalled by a commercial aired during the Olympics that depicted graphic violence, an organization that opposes media violence wrote to television station executives, demanding that the commercial be taken off the air. Letters were sent to the federal agency that oversees telecommunications, the local station that aired the commercial, and the sponsor of the advertisement. The letters explained that the commercial was inappropriate in general but especially offensive when aired as part of a special televised event intended to attract viewers of all ages.

Where do I fit in?

With so many different forms of advocacy, you may ask, Where do I fit in? How can I make a difference for children and for families? The simple answer is: wherever you are most comfortable focusing on the early childhood issues you feel most passionate about (see "Actions Early Childhood Advocates Can Take" for a range of starting places). Chances are, once you get started down the road of advocacy, your interest in a particular issue, the ease with which you define the issue, and the number of solutions you offer to resolve the issue will grow exponentially. You may ultimately find yourself engaging in all three kinds of advocacy.

Just as there are many different *forms* of advocacy, there are also many different *levels* of advocacy. Some advocates will be leaders—people who provide vision and keep the advocacy effort on track. Other advocates will be advisors—people who are willing to share their special expertise with advocates and the policymakers that advocates are trying to influence. Some will be researchers—people who can collect data and synthesize research reports into issue briefs and background papers. Still other advocates will be "contributors"—those

Parents Speak Out and Achieve Positive Results for the

Parent Voices is a grassroots parent-run program that provides a way for parents to help increase funding for, improve quality of, and provide better access to child care, particularly for working families with low incomes. The program was organized in 1996 when several resource-and-referral agencies in Northern California realized it was necessary to have parents represented at the table when decisions about child care were being made. Since that time, Parent Voices has made invaluable contributions at the state and local level, influencing policy and funding decisions to help working families with low incomes and their children.

There are three local Parent Voices chapters in the San Francisco Bay area. Each chapter sets and pursues its own advocacy agenda. In addition, chapters come together to work on statewide public policy issues that are coordinated by the California Child Care Resource and Referral Network.

Parent Voices makes its stand by

• conducting formal training sessions for parents on how to be effective advocates for their cause

• providing information to parents about how they can contact their elected officials to ensure their voices are heard

• organizing letter-writing campaigns

• visiting their legislators' offices to garner support for child care legislation

• organizing child care program site visits for their elected officials

• testifying at legislative hearings on the impact of child care support and Proposition 10, the California Children and Families First Program that provides funds to counties for establishment of comprehensive early childhood development and smoking prevention programs

• supporting or endorsing bills

• organizing annual Stand for Children rallies at the state capitol in Sacramento

Accomplishments

The following are some accomplishments of Parent Voices:

increasing public awareness about the child care needs of working parents with low incomes. Parent Voices participated in a Green Light Vigil on the steps of the state capitol to highlight the child care needs of working families with low incomes and the child care staffing crisis. First names of children on the waiting list for child care were read to demonstrate the huge number of

Child Care Needs of Working Families with Low Incomes

children eligible and not being served. In addition, parents made paper dolls to distribute to every state legislator to call further attention to the lack of available subsidized child care slots. The dolls reflected the diversity of families, nationalities, races, and ages. Legislators were given first names and stories that told of the families' budgets, situations, time on the waiting list, and other facts reflective of their community.

• *educating state policymakers.* More than 120 parents participated in a Parent Voices Legislative Action Day in Sacramento to educate state policymakers about child care issues.

• *increasing state funding for child care.* In partnership with the Women's Legislative Caucus, Parent Voices was responsible for getting a $134 million child care package passed by the state legislature during fiscal year 2000. In addition, when parents were on the verge of being terminated from CalWORKS Stage Three child care due to a shortfall of funds, Parent Voices campaigned and got the state legislature to provide the $50 million needed to fulfill its commitment to families transitioning off welfare.

• *expanding before- and after-school care opportunities in Sacramento.* Members of Parent Voices in Sacramento won an agreement with the Sacramento Unified School District to expand before- and after-school child care in the district's elementary schools.

• *instituting meaningful parent involvement in San Francisco.* Parent involvement was taken to another level when the Parent Voices chapter in San Francisco advocated to get the city to pass a requirement that every city committee making decisions on family issues include parents on the committee and in the deliberations.

Lessons learned

The following were among the lessons learned by Parent Voices:

• Legislators really listen to parents.

• Parents have compelling stories to tell and want to share them to influence policymakers.

• Sometimes it is difficult to get parents to show up for monthly meetings, but when you need them for an event, they are always there to help and are sure to be articulate and effective in conveying their message.

Based on a telephone interview in December 2000 with Melinda Felice, Parent Voices lead coordinator.

people who are willing to roll up their sleeves and participate in the nuts-and-bolts work of advocacy, from making phone calls to stuffing letters or marching in front of the state capitol. And others will be friends—people who who do not have the time or resources to participate in every aspect of the planning and implementation of advocacy, yet who care and can always be counted on to help when a push is needed. Recognize that you may move among these different levels at different times, and that your participation is always welcome and useful.

Focus your efforts

In early childhood advocacy, finding your voice and keeping focused is essential. It can be discouraging when change is not immediate, but advocacy is a slow and incremental process. As long as you speak up and stay on target, you will feel comfortable and confident in your advocacy, unflinching when confronting others and undeterred from your commitment. Enjoy your involvement and know that children will benefit from your willingness to speak out on their behalf.

Increasing Compensation for Early Childhood Professionals

North Carolina recognizes that to build and maintain a quality early care and education workforce, the state must compensate providers for additional education and training. The T.E.A.C.H.® (Teacher Education and Compensation Helps) Early Childhood Project was created in response to a 1989 North Carolina workforce study that examined the wages and retention of child care workers. Concerned about the findings, Child Care Services Association of North Carolina—a nonprofit service, research, and advocacy group—designed the project. It is now being replicated in eight states across the country.

Started as a small pilot project in 1990 with 21 participants and $23,100 from five different funding sources, T.E.A.C.H.® grew into a statewide initiative offering financial support each year to thousands of child care providers who care for children in state-regulated settings and who complete course work in early childhood education. In 2001, $2.8 million supported nearly 5,000 scholarship recipients in North Carolina. This funding came from a mixture of state dollars and private funds.

T.E.A.C.H.® works to improve the quality of care and reduce turnover by increasing access to education and providing more compensation for early childhood professionals.

Available to everyone working in a state-regulated child care program, scholarships allow early childhood professionals to work toward a North Carolina Early Childhood Credential, a North Carolina Early Childhood Administration Credential, a Child Development Associate (CDA) Credential, an associate's or bachelor's degree in early childhood education, or a North Carolina Childhood Model/Mentor Teacher standing.

T.E.A.C.H.® expects child care programs to support the continuing education of their staff by offering release time and providing increased compensation (in the form of a bonus) that is directly related to better education. In exchange for these benefits, participants make a commitment to remain in their child care setting or the field for a specified period after their scholarship year.

Designing and implementing T.E.A.C.H.® required strategic political advocacy. The following are some of the highlights of the approach to advocacy in North Carolina:

• *compiling sound research.* From the earliest days the advocates used research to educate benefactors about the conditions of the child care workforce and what quality and stability of the workforce mean to child development. Research continues and is useful when the state legislature reconsiders funding levels for the project.

• **securing support of the gubernatorial candidate.** Some early care and education leaders worked with Governor Hunt prior to his 1992 campaign and were able to convince him that early childhood education is important and that, in particular, addressing the workforce issues would be critical. Governor Hunt made early childhood education a key component of his campaign and, once elected, he allocated the first $1 million of state money from his budget for the T.E.A.C.H.® project.

• **instituting letter-writing campaigns.** T.E.A.C.H.® reminds recipients to send thank-you letters to the governor and their state legislators. These letters remind the politicians that the program is having an impact on the child care workforce and on their own constituents.

• **offering public testimony.** Advocates for and recipients of the scholarships are always available to testify during a legislative hearing at the statehouse or to meet one-on-one with legislators to share research about the child care work force and talk about accomplishments. Recipients explain how the opportunity benefited them and the children in their care.

• **instituting links to state colleges and universities.** The designers were thinking strategically when they decided that the scholarships should be used only within North Carolina's state colleges and universities. For the benefactors, especially the state legislators, knowing that the funds are being reinvested in state schools is a benefit.

• **lobbying.** The statewide child care coalition supported T.E.A.C.H.® and put a full-time lobbyist to work on building the political support needed.

All of this effort to build public and political support has been so successful that T.E.A.C.H.® is now a recurring item in the state budget.

Accomplishments

T.E.A.C.H.® has accomplished the following:

• **reducing turnover.** Turnover in regulated child care programs has been reduced from 42 to 31 percent.

• **reaching a large segment of early childhood professionals.** More than one-third of licensed centers in North Carolina have at least one T.E.A.C.H.® scholarship participant.

• **increasing earnings of early childhood professionals.** Scholarship recipients average 13 credit hours a year and increase their earnings working toward an AAS in early childhood education at a rate of 10 percent per year.

• **modeling an effective compensation program for the country.** As of November 2000, the T.E.A.C.H.® program had been replicated in eight states. Several other states are soon

(continued on p. 22)

Increasing Compensation for Early Childhood Professionals (cont'd)

to join the effort. In 2001 these states are expected to spend approximately $17.2 million, offering more than 13,500 scholarships nationwide. This involves the participation of more than 400 colleges and universities.

• promoting systems change. T.E.A.C.H® has prompted system changes in North Carolina. For example, family child care providers expressed the concern that no courses offered by the community colleges focused on their particular issues. As a result the North Carolina Family Child Care Credential was developed. In addition, feedback from recipients lead community colleges to offer more night and weekend classes to make it easier for scholarship recipients to take classes. Further, it is widely understood that because of T.E.A.C.H.®, North Carolina's efforts to establish minimum education standards for teachers and directors were successful.

Lessons learned

T.E.A.C.H.® learned the following lessons from its experiences:

• Research and share data. It is critical to use data to demonstrate the need for addressing child care workforce issues so that benefactors will understand and be willing to contribute resources. Data also are important for illustrating how the investments pay off—who is being served, how the service is changing practice, what difference it is making for children, and so on.

• Furnish sufficient incentives for child care providers to want to participate in a scholarship program. Giving tuition assistance is not enough. Thought needs to be given to how the scholarship recipient can balance work, family, and continuing education. Thus, any approach to addressing compensation through increased education needs to offer comprehensive supports (e.g., release time, transportation, books, and so on) and a bonus or raise when the scholarship recipient has successfully completed an agreed-upon amount of course work.

• Start small to test the approach and build early successes. Ensure adequate time to work with the community colleges so that they can be prepared to serve early childhood professionals.

• Be inclusive and collaborate with community colleges, universities, child care resource-and-referral agencies, Head Start, child care centers, family child care providers, and others.

• Blend public and private funding to establish broad support for the project.

Based on a telephone interview in January 2001 with Sue Russell, executive director of the Child Care Services Association of North Carolina.

CHAPTER 2

Building Capacity

Effective advocacy, especially policy advocacy, requires vision, commitment, stamina, and optimism. Good advocacy is more of an art than a science. The most successful advocates know when to alter a strategy, reach out to nontraditional partners, and recreate materials to speak differently to diverse audiences. They know when to push harder and when to be silent. They know when to provide background information, when to be persuasive, how to use data and anecdotes, and how to collaborate with others to provide a unified message with a larger number of voices.

Gains often are made through incremental victories. Advocates celebrate those victories, even though small, as foundations for the next step toward a long-term vision.

Advocacy is about persuasion. A policymaker may be well informed and yet still not vote for or propose policies that your group knows are in the best interests of children or the early childhood profession. He or she must be persuaded. Advocacy is active, not passive. Frederick Douglass said, "Power concedes nothing without a demand."

Effective advocacy consists of plans and actions that are

❖ *intentional.* You and your coalition or organization know what you are seeking to accomplish, and plan accordingly.

❖ *strategic.* You take into account the political climate in which you are working and the ability of your organization to financially and emotionally sustain the advocacy effort as it builds to its conclusion.

❖ *flexible.* You foster the ability to adjust your plans, tools, and actions as needed. For example, you add new partners when it is necessary to do so, negotiate the language of a bill, and create new materials for different audiences.

❖ *organized.* You identify the issue succinctly for your audiences, compile facts, create the materials needed to inform others of the issue and the proposed solution, and organize yourselves and others around your purpose and goals.

Getting organized

Commitment, a desire to speak out, and an organized effort are the beginnings of effective policy adocacy. There must be people in place who can make decisions, do the analysis and write, grow a well-informed grassroots network, and even people who prompt others to take quick action. Partnerships must be forged with others who share your concerns and are willing to speak out on the issues. All of these elements are crucial, regardless of the topic selected.

Advocacy for changes in policy or increased resources—whether at the federal, state, or local level—requires organizations and individuals to work in concert on the same goal and with the same strategy. Too many times, people speak out without first finding out what other early childhood advocates are doing. If you or your organization do not try to work together with others, policymakers will be ready to divide opinions and hold on to the status quo.

Here are some steps in building capacity to initiate and sustain advocacy of well-defined goals.

Creating a proactive agenda

Creating an agenda is the next step in outlining an advocacy campaign after laying the organizational groundwork. Your organization must define both its long-term and short-term vision as well as its priorities among multiple issues. Your definitions must reflect what can realistically be accomplished in each case.

Establishing a Public Policy Advocacy Committee

One way a group can realize its commitment to advocacy is by establishing a public policy committee. A policy committee communicates regularly with its members; provides a focus for gathering, analyzing, and sharing information broadly; and plans and organizes the distribution of information and the activities relating to advocacy.

The committee should designate a chairperson, a leader who has the time, interest, and skills to support the committee as a whole. A good chair delegates responsibility so that the other members of the committee can contribute according to their abilities and talents.

A policy committee interacts with the governing board of the advocacy organization, taking up and researching issues and presenting recommendations for action. The committee may draft resolutions, policy briefs, or position statements for adoption by the board.

• *Position statements* are summaries of evidence, together with conclusions and recommendations.[1] They usually include a rationale, definitions of frequently used terms, a review of relevant literature, recommendations for change, and references. Position statements provide a framework for further action on an issue, such as sending letters to legislators or newspaper editors, responding to proposed regulations, or preparing testimony. For example, NAEYC has position statements on a number of critical issues in the field of early childhood education, such as standardized testing. NAEYC's position statements include a description of the issue or problem and a discussion of the research on that topic.

• In contrast to position statements, *policy briefs* are meant to be used as advocacy guides. As the name suggests, they tend to be brief and broad enough so that an organization or coalition can support its stance on a piece of legislation. A policy brief is less academic in style than a position statement.

Source: Adapted, by permission of the authors, from S. Goffin & J. Lombardi, *Speaking Out: Early Childhood Advocacy* (Washington, DC: NAEYC, 1988), 66–68.

Training Early Childhood Community Leaders in Nebraska

In 2000, Nebraska embarked on an effort called "Taking the Lead: Building Early Childhood Community Leaders." A training institute, Taking the Lead is dedicated to meeting the growing need for leadership to represent children and families in public decisionmaking. Paid for in part through federal child care development block-grant quality dollars and implemented by the Early Childhood Training Center, the institute is building a cadre of leaders in Nebraska who recognize the value of speaking out about the importance of high-quality early care and education.

Sixty-nine people have participated in the training. Nominated by the early childhood education professional organizations in the state (e.g., NE AEYC, NE Family Child Care Association, NE Head Start, and the state Council for Exceptional Children) as well as each of the 14 regional early childhood training coalitions, participants come from a variety of settings, including child care homes and centers, Head Start programs, and community-based child care programs. Several policymakers from the state Departments of Education and Health and Human Services also have taken the training.

The five-day program conducted by the institute is divided into two two-and-a-half-day sessions each year. The sessions are designed to help participants

• learn skills that empower them,

• discover their leadership abilities,

• deal effectively with people and bureaucracies,

• take part in the public-policy process,

• exert a powerful influence in the community, and

• change the issues affecting children and families.

Topics run the gamut from helping participants understand their personal leadership style to effectively designing and facilitating a meeting to creating a vision and developing an action plan. Tips are given on becoming involved with public policy, analyzing issues, demonstrating ethical leadership, and working with the media.

The institute is more than a one-shot training session. Coaches and mentors continue to work with participants after the training. Participants are invited to identify the activities they are most interested in (e.g., public policy, public awareness, writing skills, training, business partnerships, and leadership in professional organizations or committees), and opportunities are then created for them to work with the institute staff on those activities. For example, trainees who express an interest in public policy receive notices from their coach about opportunities for testifying or writing letters to the state legislature. Background material is provided so that participants have the data and resources they need to make a compelling case.

Accomplishments

Taking the Lead has accomplished the following:

• *reviving interest, commitment, and passion for early childhood care and education.* Many child care and early education providers have become discouraged because Nebraska's investment in early childhood is quite limited. But the training institute is helping to revive interest, commitment, and passion, re-energizing those who work within the field and increasing public understanding about and commitment to quality care and education for children.

• *creating a network with other early childhood professionals.* A listserve distribution list helps keep participants at the training institute connected throughout the year. This networking allows them to share ideas, find solutions to common problems, and work together on behalf of the children they serve.

• *increasing comfort with and participation in the political process.* Participants leave the institute feeling empowered, informed, and better able to take part in the political process in Nebraska. For example, they offer testimony at legislative hearings and write letters to legislators.

• *attracting more media coverage of early childhood issues.* The number of stories addressing early childhood in state and local newspapers has increased.

• *promoting more effective meetings.* Many participants report that as a result of their training at the institute, they are able to design and carry out more effective meetings. They are better able to structure an agenda, seek input, and communicate collaboratively.

Lessons learned

Through its operation of the institute, Taking the Lead has learned the following lessons:

• Collaborating across disciplines is important in developing a leadership training institute. The early care and education community in Nebraska collaborated with the cooperative ex-

(continued on p. 28)

tension program, which had success-fully developed and delivered a lead-ership training outline. The groups worked together to modify the training so that it would address early childhood needs and issues.

• Going slow early on may be neces-sary in order to go fast later. Taking on a project such as the establish-ment of a training institute can be discouraging at times, but if you keep with it and stay focused, it will come together and the benefits will be realized.

• Staying connected with the re-search base provides a good founda-tion on which to build.

• Coming back to and checking your desired outcomes helps you see if you are achieving them.

• Following up with participants en-ables you to stay connected with them and affords them opportunities to share their success stories. Send-ing regular reminders, calling indi-vidual participants, or setting up some other mechanism for commu-nication helps sustain momentum and share successes.

Based on a January 2001 telephone interview with Carol Fichter, director of the Nebraska Early Childhood Training Center.

Sometimes the task of prioritizing issues for advocacy at the federal, state, or local level seems overwhelming. Your group may have posi-tions allowing you to support a wide range of public policies affecting early childhood education in your community, but you need to select only those issues of the most pressing concern and those that can be advanced with some potential for success in the current political con-text. In addition, consider a long-term goal for certain issues. Expediency should not be the only concern; each attempt to promote and secure good public policies, whether successful or not, should build on previous efforts and make the achievement of long-term goals more likely.

Define the problem, frame the issue

It is important to define your group's focus within the context of your vision of what a high-quality system of early childhood education should look like for *all* children. On the basis of that vision, identify problems with the current system or a part thereof and examine the root causes of those problems. For example, early childhood education programs experience high turnover rates because they usually cannot pay their employees well. Here the larger issue is the recruitment and retention of qualified and well-compensated early childhood staff. Similarly, if the particular problem is that people routinely leave trash strewn at the neighborhood playground, then the broader issue is protecting children's health and safety.

Short-term and long-term goals

The political climate in Congress, in the state legislature, and in the local school board or community will influence your decision regarding the scope of the agenda to pursue in the short-term and the long-term. If a large program is being reauthorized, that is a significant part of the context in which your group will work, even if it does not mesh with your proactive agenda. A governor's agenda and budget proposal establishes an inevitable blueprint for action areas. Whether you are in an election year can be a help or a hindrance, depending on whether polling shows your issues to be of concern to a large number of voters. Do larger interests set by both political parties make it difficult to find a champion this year on a particular issue? If the party in control has set health care as its priority, can you frame your issue in a way that connects to this highlighted issue? For example, you can turn your agenda on violence in children's lives into a health issue. This is when having a proactive agenda is particularly important; a positive message stating what should be done for young children can connect your issue to the short-term political context as well as keep you on track for longer term goals.

Find the right forum

As you develop an agenda, your group should determine whether the federal, state, or local level is the best one in which to move it. Is the issue one that should be tackled through legislation, regulation, or private partnerships? Many things are accomplished not through legislation but through regulation, particularly at the state level. In many states, legislation is written very broadly because the state's public policy tradition puts more emphasis on the regulatory processes than legislative prescriptions. Sometimes legislation exists, but the regulations are not consistent with the legislative intent or they provide so much detail that the regulations take on more practical importance than the statute. Choosing whether to target legislation or regulation depends

Advocates Secure Health Insurance for

If you are a certified home-based child care provider in Rhode Island and were paid $1,800 by the Department of Human Services for child care services within a six-month period, you and your dependent children living with you are eligible to receive health insurance coverage through RIte Care, the Rhode Island health insurance program for low-income families. In addition, licensed child care centers with more than 50 percent of their slots filled by children receiving subsidies for care are now reimbursed by the state for 50 percent of the cost of employee health coverage.

This benefit to child care providers is due to the hard work of Rhode Island advocates to make health insurance part of the 1998 Early Care and Education Initiative called Starting Right.

The road to success was long and arduous. In the early 1990s, two child care providers met at the state Department of Human Services and began talking about how the state was late in paying for their services. The women decided to draft a letter to other subsidized child care providers to see whether they too were overdue to be paid. As a result of the letter, several providers came together for a meeting and decided to go to the Department of Human Services and demand their outstanding pay. They were successful and received their pay in 10 days.

Energized by their success the providers decided to push for health coverage. Before scheduling a meeting with the department, they did extensive research to ensure that their request was reasonable and that they were prepared to answer any objections that would likely be raised.

As expected, the department's response was that the state could not afford to provide health insurance to child care providers. Undaunted, the providers hung around the halls of the department, pulling aside staff and asking them if they had health insurance and how they felt about it. They used the opportunity to tell the

in large part on your state or local community's traditions in making and enforcing public policy.

Learn "how things get done," that is, the process for legislative, regulatory, and executive policymaking. In addition to the process, learn about the personalities: who is a leader, a bridge builder, a partisan fighter, a "behind the scenes" negotiator, or an attention-seeker. At

Child Care Providers in Rhode Island

workers that child care providers lacked health insurance and that the department wouldn't consider offering it to them.

The number of child care workers grew and their voices were heard. With the support of Direct Action for Rights and Equality (DARE), a non-profit community-organizing group, they continued to apply pressure at the state level. After several meetings with department officials and state legislators, even the governor, their patience and persistence prevailed, and they secured health insurance as a right for many child care providers in Rhode Island.

Accomplishments

RIte Care succeeded in:

• securing health coverage for child care providers. As of October 1999, 189 home-based child care providers and 163 dependent children were covered in the state. An additional 279 employees working at 26 licensed centers, each with more than 50 percent of the children it served receiving state subsidies, also obtained coverage.

Lessons learned

RIte Care learned the following lessons from its experience with the Department of Human Services:

• Meet frequently with your peers to talk through issues, and reach a group decision about what you want and how you will pursue it.

• Do your research in advance so that you are prepared to make a persuasive argument and can answer the questions that will be raised.

• Listen to those from whom you need support. Listening carefully shows respect and helps you better understand their arguments and how you can best respond to them.

• Be persistent.

Based on a telephone interview in January 2001 with Shirley Craighead, a home-based child care provider in Rhode Island.

different times as you pursue your agenda, certain personalities will be more effective champions.

In other circumstances, using the political process is either premature or simply not feasible for reaching your desired result. In that case, you should consider private partnerships or public engagement to create the base of support you may need later for a public policy solution.

Developing the message

Determining how to frame an issue is critical. There are several audiences for your project: your base of supporters, likely coalition members, and policymakers you are trying to influence. The press, community leaders, and the general public may also be part of your strategic audiences. The way you talk about the issue with the public, the press, and legislators must be consistent and persuasive. How you frame the issue and the language you use to convey it is commonly known as the *message*.

The message of your advocacy activity should be clear and simple. If it takes more than two or three sentences to state your message, you need to break it down into several different messages. Effective communication with policymakers, the media, and the public will depend on your consistent use of the message. Always express the message in a way that best fits your intended audience, whether it be federal policymakers, state boards, local community groups, business executives, or parents.

Sometimes it is easy to decide how to phrase the message. One way to check whether it will resonate with the public is to look at outside information, such as polling and focus group results. Many polls are made public on the Internet and in newspapers. Polls and focus groups can help you frame the language you need to persuade a particular audience. For example, would you get a better response if you used the phrase "with government funds" rather than "with public funds"? If you used the phrase "early learning" rather than "child care"?

Working with others—Expanding your partnerships

Rarely is it effective for a group to work alone, especially in policy advocacy. The most powerful coalitions are often those that combine groups that are traditionally not seen as direct stakeholders in the advocacy effort. Too often, advocates are fearful of reaching out beyond those organizations with which they have longstanding professional relationships. Ask yourself: Who is already engaged in this issue? Who can bring additional resources (not just financial), clout, or expertise, to your effort? Have you reached out to community health centers, nurses, disability advocates, organized labor, business, or industry? Not all of these organizations or entities are the right partners for every advocacy effort, but reaching out to nontraditional partners at the right time for the right activity can give you new momentum and raise your likelihood of success.

The more formal and stable a coalition, the more effective it will be. The group should hold regular meetings. Many times, you will meet simply to share information. Even if there is little news, you should continue to meet to keep everyone connected to each other and to the shared agenda. Most networks are informal groups that meet regularly to share information. No advocate attends every meeting. However, every organization should designate one or more representatives who will commit to attending these network meetings on a regular basis.

Choosing your partners is an important part of your strategic plan. The most obvious method of forming a coalition is to identify other groups who share similar interests. They may share all of your interests or only some of them. As long as there is some common objective shared by all the groups, the potential exists to form a coalition.

Here are some partners to consider:

Parents. Working with parents is very important, and supporting them as advocates should be part of your agenda. Early childhood education has a long tradition of parent involvement as a cornerstone of high-quality programs and schools. Because parents are a child's first advocates, they often make good advocates for all of the children in the community. Organized, they are a very powerful voice.

Parents are also an authentic voice seeking quality child care and school reform. From the mayor and the school board to members of Congress, public officials treat parents not only as concerned citizens but also as influential constituents. For example, local and state PTAs work with many other organizations to improve nonschool-based services, such as libraries and child health care, as well as school reform issues like teacher quality and testing. Parents also are influential in supporting improvement of working conditions and policies.

Health care practitioners, law enforcement officials, and other professionals. Having professionals in other fields as partners shows that your agenda is not motivated by self-interest. Such professionals can provide you with more data, expert witnesses on a range of topics, and connections to other families and community leaders. For example, Fight Crime: Invest in Kids is a national organization of police officers

Early Care and Education Community in Maine Comes

Faced with a budget shortfall of $300 million for fiscal year 2001, term limits ushering out legislators who are knowledgeable about the child care resources and needs in the state, and an administration whose diminishing size and resources jeopardize the child care needs of families, the child care community in Maine is working ever more vigilantly to combine the efforts of its various constituents to support the systemic changes needed to build access to quality child care.

In the mid-1990s, three agencies—the Maine Child Care Directors Association, the Maine Head Start Directors Association, and the Maine Association of Child Care Resource and Referral Agencies—came together with a desire to educate the state about quality child care. The three formed the Alliance for Children's Care, Education, and Supporting Services (ACCESS), an organized body of early care and education providers and advocates whose mission is to ensure the availability of family-focused services through collaborative relationships with traditional and nontraditional partners.

Today Maine has a statewide AC-CESS Steering Committee that meets twice monthly, statewide standing committees (dealing with assessment, professional development, public policy, business and economic development, and resource development, among other things), and 11 local ACCESS collaborations comprised of parents, child care providers of all varieties (e.g., for-profit and nonprofit agencies, extended families, family child care and services), public schools, the local education agency, businesses, and many other entities.

Recognizing that the whole is greater than any of its parts, the early care and education community in Maine uses ACCESS as a vehicle for working collaboratively to increase awareness about child care issues and to push for the changes needed to increase access to quality care. Rather than one program competing against another for the same pot of funds, programs come together to determine which is the best candidate for the particular funds, with an eye toward supporting and expanding existing programs but also nurturing new and emerging providers. This collaborative nature helps the field stay focused and expand, even in challenging political and financial times.

Together to Support Systemic Changes

Accomplishments

Among the accomplishments of ACCESS and the local collaboratives are the following:

• *securing additional state resources for early care and education.* ACCESS can take shared responsibility for the success of the Start ME Right early care and education initiative in Maine. Nearly a dozen bills have passed that support the initiative, including legislation that increased funding for subsidized child care, expanded Head Start to a full-day, full-year program, expanded statewide voluntary home-visiting programs, and provided funds for quality improvements. Legislation also passed that seeded an ongoing revolving loan fund for child care providers and a tuition assistance plan to encourage providers to continue their education. Further, a new state law doubles a parent's child care tax credit if the child is enrolled in an accredited program and doubles an employer's tax credit if the employer creates an accredited child care program for employees.

• *focusing on children with special needs.* A local collaborative hosted a meeting on the challenges of providing care to children with special needs and the systemic changes needed so that services could be more available and appropriate for these children.

• *educating state legislators.* The Kennebec Somerset ACCESS Collaborative collects data on child care resources and needs and creates brochures tailored to the elected state legislators in a two-county area. The brochures are mailed to legislators, and follow-up meetings are held in which local child care providers call on their state legislator to discuss the brochure topics and local child care issues. Continuing to ensure that legislators understand child care issues is a challenge now that term limits are in force, but this strategy has proven successful and thus will continue.

• *initiating discussions with the business community.* With an influx of new companies interested in building business parks in Maine, the child care community is initiating discussions with the business community to help businesses understand the child care issues that are important to worker productivity. Discussions focus on access, affordability, and quality, with the aim of engaging various members of the business community as partners

(continued on p. 36)

with affiliates around the country that advocates for more public funding for early childhood education and after-school programs. They add credibility to your coalition's goals because their members are not considered direct beneficiaries of the availability and quality of child care.

Community-based and faith-based organizations. By including community-based and faith-based organizations in your advocacy efforts, you build a larger network of organizations, especially those engaged in human or social services, who share your concerns and can learn new ways to deal with the issues. These organizations can disseminate your information in their newsletters and help find stories about the advocacy efforts of people in the community that can bring the problem, as well as solutions, into sharp focus.

Business and union partners

Both business and labor have a stake in child care, education, and families' economic stability. To them, the issue is more than just preparing children for school; it is also about the readiness of the future workforce. The early years are important in preparing children to become good thinkers, skills they will need in the workplace.

Businesses and labor unions have resources that may not be available in your volunteer early childhood advocacy network. For example, their organizations' staffs include public-relations and technology experts, and often lobbyists. They may allow some of these experts to volunteer their services to your organization or coalition, or they may even become a partner in your efforts.

Business. In every community, in every state, and at the national level, small and large business leaders can be strong allies in advocacy efforts. Their participation can run the gamut from sponsoring town hall meetings and other public-awareness events to lobbying the governor or the legislature for public funding and new initiatives.

There are a number of sound reasons for engaging the business community:

❖ When business leaders speak, people—especially policymakers—listen. The public's perception is that business leaders understand good investments and avoid "waste."

❖ Business leaders are unexpected messengers on issues dealing with children and families. Policymakers are used to business leaders talking about economic incentives, tax credits, and expansion loans, not about children. Accordingly, business is not viewed as interested in matters relating to young children, which is a plus for your advocacy efforts.

❖ Business leaders often have political and media contacts that early childhood and education advocates have not been able to reach or convince. They work with different staff in the policymakers' offices and can reach newspaper and other reporters who deal with business issues, contacts that you would not otherwise be able to reach.

Recruiting business leaders and engaging them in your advocacy activities is worth the effort if you are strategic in your approach. Depending on the kind of advocacy you are conducting, different choices must be made about the business leaders to approach. You must make a case for why the business should be involved in your efforts. For example, if you are working on a public policy issue, identify business leaders who already have the ear of the governor or of important leaders in the state legislature or council. As Blood and Ludtke suggest, find leaders who are part of the state or community's *political cognoscenti*, a group of opinion leaders who "absolutely drive thinking" on policy issues.[2]

You will also need to think differently about how business leaders become involved in advocacy, compared to other stakeholders that participate in your efforts. Business leaders may want to form their own task force, not send representatives to yours. In other instances, they may want to be a part of the coalition. Either method helps bring your message to important decisionmakers, although you may not be in the room.

The Pennsylvania Partnership for Children has experience with creating business advocacy in support of a statewide preschool initiative. Here are some lessons it has learned[3]:

❖ Business sets the pace for its involvement.

❖ Advocates should not go into the process harboring preconceptions about why business is interested.

❖ Businesspeople want facts, data, and research results so they can understand the issues before speaking to them.

❖ Business often transpires behind closed doors, with very little exposure to the public. It may be hard for advocates to gain information.

❖ Advocates should learn business language; getting to know staffs will enable advocates to understand how business "talks."

❖ Businesspeople want results and accountability, so advocates should work with that in mind.

❖ An early childhood initiative may not be the top priority of businesspeople, and it may be put on a back burner.

❖ Businesspeople will give you credit when you need it.

❖ Advocates should keep thanking business leaders for opening doors and for making their resources available.

For other advocacy goals, your group may want to focus on business leaders who contributed time or money to sponsor certain kinds of nonprofit groups (e.g., hospitals, clinics, or schools) or family-friendly events in the past. These leaders may never have been invited to sponsor a breakfast or community event—for example, the Week of the Young Child—but by offering them the opportunity to do so, you establish a connection to them for other activities and efforts in the future. Then, as the relationship grows, you can ask them to recruit other businesses to join in your efforts.

Business leaders will not have the expertise that you have regarding issues relating to young children and families. It is your job to keep those leaders informed and to provide them with the knowledge they need to put forward arguments that lead to desired results. Present them with a lot of information; they use facts and numbers every day and depend on them. Your job is to provide good, solid data, to explain the importance of quality care and education and what makes high-quality programs, and to highlight the urgency of giving families access to child care that meets their needs.

Labor unions. Unions have taken on issues of pay equity and workplace conditions that intersect with early childhood education concerns. Several unions have a long history of working on public policies to support well-funded, quality child care and public schools and paid family leave. Unions also respond to their members' needs by negotiating child care assistance benefits in employment contracts.

As with the business community, there are a number of reasons for engaging labor unions in your advocacy.

❖ Labor unions have a history of advocating for better pay, family and medical leave, and other social issues at the state and national level.

❖ They know how to organize people, whether it be recruiting new members to rallying members around an activity or issue.

❖ Unions have at least one full-time lobbyist and a public relations expert—and sometimes many more—in each state affiliate.

❖ Labor unions represent millions of workers and support not only issues that affect their members directly, such as access to affordable, quality child care, but also those affecting the working conditions of other workers, such as child care staff.

❖ Because labor unions do campaign work, they conduct polling and focus groups and often have access to media that will enlarge your coalition's efforts.

Building a Solid Coalition

Coalitions are outcome oriented and are only as strong as their member organizations' skills, contacts, and commitment. Intense efforts are required to create and maintain a shared focus. Therefore, strong leadership, sufficient resources, and a steady eye on the desired outcome are necessary for a coalition's success.[4]

Successful legislative campaigns depend on the active participation of a large and diverse constituency that sends a message of broad-based support to decisionmakers. Coalitions should include as many organizations as possible that share an interest in a particular legislative issue, although the reasons for their interest may vary. A coalition's strength comes from its ability to activate a large number of advocates and to propose concrete initiatives in ways that unorganized constituencies cannot.[5]

To create and maintain a shared focus, coalition members must be able to put aside their differences and concentrate on the desired outcome—not always an easy task. Participants need to be skilled in negotiation and compromise; people are likely to disagree on priorities, strategies, and tactics. The effort required to resolve differences is worthwhile, because of the greater political impact of organized constituencies.

Coalition organizers often need to convince potential participants of the advantage of their involvement and reassure them that the coalition will not take over any of their present functions.[6] Each group should be approached with arguments based on its own interests. In Indiana, for example, advocates for school-age child care legislation won the support of local fire officials and county prosecutors by arguing that unsupervised children were more likely to hurt themselves and others than were children in supervised programs.[7]

A considerable leadership effort is needed to maintain members' involvement, sustain their motivation, and unite their efforts. Groups must be clear about what contributions they are expected to make and the issues they support. No group should be pushed to go beyond its resources or interests. Regular communication and opportunities for members to influence group decisions are crucial. Members should receive sincere, meaningful recognition.

Source: Reprinted, by permission of the authors, from S. Goffin & J. Lombardi, *Speaking Out: Early Childhood Advocacy* (Washington, DC: NAEYC, 1988), 69, 71.

Many of the "lessons learned" by advocates working with business leaders are applicable to working with unions. Many unions have been involved in education and child care efforts at the national and state levels. In addition to teachers' unions, the United Auto Workers, the American Federation of State, County and Municipal Employees, and the Service Employees International Union have worked in coalitions to advance child care assistance, higher funding levels for schools in low-income communities, professional development for teachers, and other education initiatives. Labor unions also are proven allies in many child care public policy campaigns. For example, the Labor Project for Working Families, a group of unions, advocates, and community groups in San Francisco, designed an agenda known as the Work and Family Bill of Rights, including the CARES bill (a child care workforce compensation initiative) to improve the compensation of child care staff and expand the Family and Medical Leave Act.

Endnotes

1. A.D.A. Reports, "A position paper on position papers," *Journal of the American Dietetic Association* 77 (1980): 179–181; J.C. Masters, "Models for training and research in child development and social policy," *Annals of child development* Vol.1, ed. G.J. Whitehurst (Greenwich, CT: JAI Press, 1984).
2. M. Blood, & M. Ludtke, *Business leaders as legislative advocates for children* (New York: Foundation for Child Development, 1999).
3. Adapted from J. Benso, presentation at the 2001 NAEYC Leadership Conference, 9 June 2001 (Washington, DC).
4. S.R. Bing, & D.W. Richart, *Fairness is a kid's game: A background paper for child advocates* (Indianapolis: The Lilly Endowment, Inc., 1987).
5. C.D. Hayes, ed., *Making policies for children: A study of the federal process* (Washington, DC: National Academic Press, 1982).
6. M. Fried, "Coalition building for children," *Young Children* 38, no. 4 (1983): 77–80.
7. A. Wilkins, & H. Bank, "Child care: Strategies to move the issue forward," *Young Children* 42, no. 1 (1986): 68–72.

CHAPTER 3

Knowing and Using the Legislative and Regulatory Processes

In trying to increase access to and improve the quality of early childhood education, advocates will find that much of their work involves federal and state legislation and regulations. Outside of parent fees, the funding for child care, Head Start, and programs focused on helping children in low-income schools primarily comes from federal and state sources. The requirements for adult-child ratios, teacher qualifications, performance standards and assessments, and other quality indicators are demands set forth in legislation or regulations.

Advocates must understand the legislative and regulatory processes and know how to use these to their advantage. This chapter provides in-depth information on these processes, using the federal legislative process as a template. Many states have the same framework for the legislative process, but each state has its own special rules and culture for legislative and regulatory work and advocates should be fluent in them as well.

Do not be daunted by details and strange terms. As you work on legislation with others who have more experience, you will find that these become less foreign. Also, expect the unexpected. Sometimes a bill's progress does not follow the typical process outlined here.

For example, there may not be a markup by the committee. The bill may appear in the form of an amendment to another piece of legislation. However, if you know the basics of the process, your efforts will continue smoothly on course.

The art of influencing public policy involves not only an understanding of the process but also of the players. The president, governor, legislators and their staffs, and agency staff all have personal and professional backgrounds and interests that influence their work on a variety of issues. Developing relationships with these people is an advocate's most important work. The most intricate understanding of the legislative process will not help advocates meet their goals if they do not know how to work well with policymakers. Therefore, this chapter begins with a discussion of how to build those critical relationships before moving to a description of the process.

Building relationships

Building a relationship with policymakers, decisionmakers, and their staffs takes effort and time. Policymakers should come to view an advocacy group as a credible, responsive source of information and ideas. Ideally, the organization will also become a sounding board for the policymaker not only on content but also on strategy.

Getting to know policymakers is not a seasonal endeavor. Advocates need to stay in touch with officials throughout the year. During certain times of the year there may not be any public action, but the agencies or the governor's office may be making plans for the next year's budget, state-of-the-state address, or public communications campaign around a particular issue that affects you and your community. By being in regular contact with a variety of policymakers, you will know in advance when action is being planned and whom you should be working with to forge relationships and effect an outcome that supports your agenda.

The officials

The next point sounds basic, but knowing something about the policymakers is the starting point for building relationships. How long have they held their current positions? Have they held other positions in elected or appointed office? Do they have a public record on the issues that concern your group? What positions do they hold in the legislature, and are they positions of seniority? What legislation that you support have they voted for or against?

Sometimes personal information helps determine how to approach a policymaker. Does the policymaker have young children or grandchildren? Is he or she a professional in a field related to your advocacy issue, such as a teacher, doctor, or social worker? An official's personal relationship to children's issues can be a point of entry for building a working relationship that will advance your goals.

Get to know your policymakers by inviting them to attend informal events, such as a visit to a child care center or school. Elected officials often hold town meetings, where you can spend more time getting to know them. Local officials often can make appointments on weekends or evenings to meet with a group.

In every contact, remember to be polite, professional, and nonpartisan. You never know when you will need a policymaker as an ally. Moreover, your reputation as an advocate depends not only on your knowledge but also on how you handle yourself with policymakers. Always be on time, always respond with promised materials, and always keep your temper in check.

The staff

Whether at the federal, state, or local level, it is aides who draft the legislation, write the memos, and negotiate the final bills. Whether senior staff or not, they are extremely important and very busy people. Yours is not the only bill on which they work, so developing a good relationship with aides is critical. Working together, you make a team. Help draft the bill, provide talking points on the issue and the bill itself, and write questions for hearings. The more you prepare the work for them, the more likely you are to get the results you want.

Always know who the critical staff are. Know the legislative director and the legislative assistant who handle your issues. Have they worked for other legislators on similar issues? Are there reasons such as previous work experience that would make him or her take a personal interest in your issues?

Understanding the legislative process

As mentioned earlier in this chapter, the federal and state legislative processes are similar but not identical. Advocates should be familiar with both. Many programs and funding streams, such as Head Start, the Child Care and Development Block Grant, and Title I of the Elementary and Secondary Education Act, are federal programs that provide grants to states, local agencies and school districts, individual programs, and parents. For example, a state's child care tiered reimbursement system may be funded by the federal Child Care and Development Block Grant.

There are different kinds of legislation. *Authorizing* legislation is legislation that creates a program, such as Head Start, and sets forth who will be the grantee, what kinds of services must be provided and to whom, and other program requirements. The legislation includes an "authorization of appropriations" paragraph. This provision states the legislature's desired funding level for the program. However, the bill's authorization appropriations do not ensure that those funding levels will be appropriated. There are also *reauthorization* bills, such as the reauthorization of the Elementary and Secondary Education Act. Originally enacted in 1965, the ESEA is now reauthorized every five years, undergoing review and change just like all other authorizing legislation.

The discretionary spending bills are known as *appropriations* bills. They are crafted and passed by committees separate from those that work on the authorizing legislation. Legislation concerning discretionary appropriations (such as bills pertaining to Head Start, child care, education, and other human services programs) is passed each year.

Nonrevenue-generating tax legislation is another kind of spending bill. Whereas an appropriation is *direct* spending on an activity or program, tax credits and deductions are *indirect* spending. That is, when an individual or business claims a credit or deduction, the federal or state treasury loses the revenue it otherwise would have collected. In essence, the government is spending money on the taxpayer through its loss of revenue. Bills to amend the tax code occur either through authorizing legislation or at the federal level as part of a budget reconciliation bill.

To influence policy, advocates must understand the different types of legislation and involve themselves in the legislative process.

An outline of the federal authorization process

Because the process of authorizing (i.e., establishing) programs at the federal level is similar to but not necessarily identical as the process used in state legislatures, you must become familiar with the rules and procedures in your state. Generally speaking, the president's role, like that of the governor of a state, is to put forward an agenda and to sign or veto legislation. These are the basic steps:

❖ A member of Congress introduces the bill, which is given an identification number.

❖ The bill is referred to one or more committees with the jurisdiction to act upon it.

❖ One or more committee hearings are held at which the bill is discussed.

❖ The committee marks up the bill and reports it out of committee.

❖ The bill is placed on the calendar for consideration by one chamber of Congress.

❖ The bill is considered in that chamber as a separate measure or as an amendment to another bill.

❖ The bill is sent to the other chamber for consideration.

❖ The House and Senate sit in conference to narrow whatever differences they have regarding the content of the bill.

❖ The bill is sent to the president for signature or veto.

❖ The president signs or vetoes the legislation; the legislature may attempt to override a veto.

An outline of the federal budget and appropriations processes

At the federal level, the budget bill sets forth a blueprint for spending and taxes. The bill does not go to the president for his signature or veto. The budget process is highly intricate and advocates need not master every complex rule. Here are some basics:

Budget request. Every February, the president submits a budget request containing both information on taxes and spending proposals. A spending amount is proposed for each federal program in every agency.

Descriptions of policy goals and programs, as well as funding figures, will be proposed for all new initiatives.

Budget resolution. The budget committees in both the House and the Senate hold hearings and introduce the budget resolution, which sets a blueprint for spending and taxes for the next five years. The budget resolution is passed each year, with amendments, by both the House and Senate, after which the two chambers convene to iron out any differences they have regarding the resolution. Interestingly, even though the House and Senate produce a final, single conference report, it is never sent to the president to sign. In other words, the budget resolution never becomes law.

Why, then, is the budget resolution important? The answer is that it sets the ceiling on spending for child care, education, health, and other policy areas of the federal government. The 13 appropriations subcommittees cannot spend more than the budget resolution allows for that year.

Reconciliation. A reconciliation bill reconciles spending needs with revenue losses (e.g., from tax cuts) set forth in the budget resolution. Sometimes the reconciliation bill calls for tax increases, other times for tax relief. Each committee that authorizes legislation must find savings for its area of jurisdiction. The recommendations from the various committees are sent to the House and Senate Budget Committees, which roll them into one budget reconciliation bill. The House and Senate then vote on the reconciliation bill and send it on to the president to sign.

Appropriations. Each Appropriations Committee is split into 13 subcommittees. The Subcommittee for Labor, Health and Human Services, and Education lists the spending amounts allocated for child care; Head Start; elementary, secondary, and higher education; labor and job training programs; health programs and health research; and social services programs such as the Low Income Home Energy Assistance Program and the Community Services Block Grant.

Because appropriating is one of the most important congressional functions, the chairs of the Appropriations Committees and subcommittees are some of the most influential members of Congress. Each subcommittee is given an allocation—a total amount of funds—that it proposes be allocated on a program-by-program basis. One of the guides for determining how much each program should receive is the amount that the authorization bill recommends, known as the "authorization of appropriations." Appropriators may not exceed that amount, and rarely even meet it in a given year.

Sometimes Congress fails to pass all of the appropriations bills by September 30, the end of the federal fiscal year. Those appropriations bills that remain unfinished require a "continuing resolution"; that is, funding authorized for programs covered by such bills continues on the basis of last fiscal year's funding levels until Congress passes the appropriations bill conference report.

State budgets

One of the most important areas for state policy advocacy is the budget process.[1] Unlike at the federal level, at the state level there are two types of budgets: operating budgets for agencies and their programs, and capital budgets for the construction or acquisition of buildings, structures, real property, and equipment. Funds for the latter generally are derived from surpluses, earmarked revenues, or the sale of bonds.

More than half of the states have an annual budget cycle that provides appropriations for one year. Twenty-three states operate on a biennial budget cycle. Some of those same states have legislatures that meet annually, but their budgets come up for review and revision only in alternating years.

The budget cycle usually begins in the summer when the state budget office sends the governor's spending targets and policy priorities to the various state agencies. This is the time for advocates to meet with state agencies and make a case for increases in programs. Coming prepared with a specific amount in mind and with items such as waiting lists to demonstrate the unmet need is helpful.

Sometime in the fall the agencies submit their requests for the next year's budget. There may be some give-and-take between the agencies and the state budget office. Finally, the state budget office analyzes the requests and puts them into a statewide proposal for the governor to consider.

The governor may change the proposal to fit his or her policy priorities. This is the time to activate your network to urge the governor to increase spending in certain programs by a specific amount. Most states

Unanimous Victory for Child Care Staff Retention in Illinois

Great START (Strategy to Attract and Retain Teachers) has an important impact on the quality of child care in Illinois. With a focus on staff retention, the program provides bonuses, based on job longevity and level of education, to licensed child care staff who remain in the field. Funding for Great START is modest—just $3 million for the first fiscal year, compared with the $25 million advocates requested—but the bipartisan commitment of the state legislature to early care and education is significant.

Concerned by the high rate of staff turnover, the fact that many people were leaving the child care field permanently for higher paying jobs in other professions, and the overall inability to staff centers across Illinois with qualified caregivers, the Day Care Action Council—a nonprofit statewide advocacy, policy, referral, and training organization— undertook a strategic planning process in 1999 to identify what could be done to address the dire situation. Those involved in the process conducted research to learn about other state efforts to increase compensation of caregivers, assessed the political climate in Illinois to determine what legislation might be possible, and expanded the grassroots network so that providers would be engaged in planning and decisionmaking.

Once a goal was identified—the introduction and passage of legislation that would raise the salaries of child care staff on the basis of their level of education and training and length of time in the field—the Day Care Action Council engaged the more than 500 members of its public policy caucus in conversations aimed at fleshing out the details.

The 2000 legislative session opened in January and was scheduled to adjourn on April 15. With little time to spare, the Day Care Action Council lobbyist and the grassroots network worked collaboratively to secure bipartisan support of legislators throughout the state. While the lobbyist worked the halls in the state capitol, the grassroots network contacted local elected officials to share stories about child care in the community and the pressing need for Great START. More than 150 people from the network participated in a lobby day and reception for legislators at the governor's mansion to talk about the issue and the legislation. The media ran child care stories across the state.

The council's efforts were supported by other important players in Illinois, especially Ounce of Prevention, Voices for Illinois Children, Fight Crime: Invest in Kids Illinois, and Chicago Metropolis 2020. Weekly fax alerts and e-mail messages kept everyone informed about the process and provided instructions for carrying out the next steps.

When the House and Senate committees reviewed the bill, the advocates orchestrated powerful testimony that convinced policymakers that Great START was a necessary investment. For example, a teacher from Rockford spoke about how she loved caring for children but did not make enough money to put milk and bread on the table for her own children. The police chief from Quincy spoke about the importance of early care and education for children. A leader from Chicago Metropolis 2020 explained why the business community was concerned about child care.

The state House and Senate passed Great START unanimously in the closing days of the legislature. The governor signed the law, and now caregivers across the state are benefiting from this step toward more adequate reimbursement for child care services.

Accomplishments

The Day Care Action Council accomplished a number of its aims:

• *galvanizing the grassroots community.* Organizers knew how important it would be to involve the grassroots community in the advocacy strategy. Accordingly, the Day Care Action Council called on its public policy caucus and other direct-service child care providers for much of the support that effectively convinced lawmakers that staff retention was an important issue for their constituents.

• *increasing awareness among policymakers of the pressing child care issues.* Direct lobbying in the state capitol by a dedicated lobbyist, combined with an organized grassroots effort to illuminate the realities of child care in local communities, was an effective strategy for helping policymakers understand child care issues.

• *securing bipartisan support.* It was vital that the Great START legislation receive bipartisan support within both the House and the Senate. Such support helped illustrate the fact that the issue was important in all communities, regardless of political persuasion.

Lessons learned

The Day Care Action Council learned at least two important lessons from its experience with Great START:

(continued on p. 52)

require the governor to submit the budget request to the state legislature. The budget request is discussed in the governor's state-of-the-state address at the start of the legislative session. The legislature's budget committees review the governor's proposal and hold hearings, with each chamber creating its own budget legislation and with the two chambers then conferring to iron out the differences between the two versions of the legislation.

Each state grants the governor different veto powers over part or all of the budget legislation. The governors of 42 states and of Puerto Rico have line-item veto authority.

Influencing each step of the process

Knowing the process is critical to knowing when and how to influence policy decisions. The next several sections set forth the fundamentals of the legislative process at the federal level and how advocates can take advantage of each step. The federal and state processes and rules are similar, and advocates should be well informed about both in order for their advocacy efforts to be most effective. (See Appendix C for more information on state government and policy.)

Step 1: Finding a champion to introduce the bill

Sometimes the president or governor is your legislative champion, offering a budget or authorizing legislation that you support. Often, advocates need to cultivate relationships with legislators to encourage them to introduce bills that move forward advocates' agendas. Several considerations arise in choosing your champion:

❖ Is the person a member of the committee that has jurisdiction over the bill?

❖ Will the legislator be able to work with members of the other political party to move the legislation forward?

❖ Will the legislator make the bill one of his or her legislative priorities for the year?

❖ Does the legislator's staff have a keen interest in, and enough experience to work on, the bill throughout the legislative process?

In your initial meetings with a legislator or his or her staff, you should discuss whether the bill will be one of the legislator's priorities for the year, whether the legislator has ideas for other bipartisan sponsors on or off the committee, and whether the legislator has any special concerns or ideas for the beginning of legislative process. Come prepared to discuss all of the reasons why this particular piece of legislation is needed. Provide as much factual information as possible; anecdotes are useful for engaging a legislator's interest, but in the end, the legislator will need to cite facts to convince other legislators that the legislation will help solve a problem that affects many children and families.

Effective advocates come to a meeting ready to present at least an outline of the legislation they are pushing. At a minimum, during the initial meeting you should be able to give your potential champion or his staff the following information about the legislation you want him or her to sponsor:

❖ What is the purpose of the bill and what problem does it address?

❖ Who would benefit?

Step 2: Introducing the bill and getting cosponsors

The legislator will send your materials to the legislative counsel of the House or Senate, who will draft the bill with all of the correct technical language. Afterward, meet with the legislative staff of your champion to make sure that both you and the legislator are satisfied with the language of the bill. You may be faced with a period of negotiation, so determine what your baseline needs are in advance of the discussion.

Once the bill is ready to be introduced, the legislator will probably make a brief written or oral statement on its behalf. Often, the legislator will issue a press release. Your organization or coalition also should issue a press release when the bill is introduced. (See Chapter 6.)

Upon its introduction, the bill will be given a bill number. At this point, you should begin seeking additional cosponsors for the legislation.

Your champion may decide to introduce the bill alone or together with other legislators. In either case, once the bill is introduced, you should continue to seek additional cosponsors. The more cosponsors you have, the better your prospects for moving the bill forward until it becomes law.

Your goal in seeking out many cosponsors is to have as many legislators as possible feel committed to the bill. It is always better to have bipartisan support. Find legislators who have a history of signing onto bills or amendments on the same general topic. Encourage constituents to call or write to potential cosponsors to request that they cosponsor the bill. Share your list of potential cosponsors with the sponsor's staff so that the staff can also contact them.

Step 3: Hearings—Getting the word out

Committees and their subcommittees hold numerous hearings during the year. Sometimes a hearing is on a specific piece of legislation; other times, the hearing is meant to provide general information about an issue. The length of hearings and the number of witnesses testifying vary. The majority and minority members of the committee can select witnesses to invite to provide oral testimony.

Committee hearings are a time to get your word out. You may be called to testify on behalf of an organization, either individually or as part of a panel of witnesses. If so, you must submit written testimony, and you must be prepared to provide your oral testimony in no more than five minutes. You may or may not be questioned by committee members. Again, check the rules if you are testifying before a state legislative committee or regulatory body.

Your written testimony can be any length and serves as a report to the committee. The written testimony should be rich with data, anecdotes (as appropriate), and comments on the proposed language of the legislation. Oral testimony is time limited, so highlight the most important points of why you support the proposed legislative solution. Be candid about any practical problems you see with the proposed legislation: just because you are in favor of the goals of a bill does not mean that it is problem free. (And, indeed, note that the suggestions made in this section apply as well to legislation you *oppose*: You still may testify at hearings, send written testimony, etc.)

Even if you are not asked to testify, most committees' rules allow individuals and organizations to submit written testimony within two weeks of the date of the hearing. Do not submit testimony just for its own sake: Make sure that you are *adding* information that would not otherwise come out in the hearing. If your points are made by other witnesses, you can send a letter to the members of the committee supporting that testimony.

This is also an opportune point in the process to work with staff. Provide them with talking points about the bill and questions for witnesses.

Step 4: Markup of the bill—Negotiating changes

The marking up of a bill is one of the most important stages in the legislative process. Markup time is when the committee offers and votes on amendments to the bill.

Generally, you will have only one week's notice that a bill is scheduled to be marked up by a subcommittee or committee. You should find out whether the chair will offer a substitute bill with substantive or only technical changes and whether any other amendments will be offered at that time. If you want changes to the bill, this is your opportunity to work with a sympathetic member of the committee.

Contact a member of the committee and let him or her know what changes your group wants and why they are important. Give the staff the exact language and where it should appear in the bill. If the member agrees to offer your amendment, send a letter of support for the amendment, preferably with the signatures of other groups in your coalition or network, to each member of the committee, urging a vote in favor of the amendment.

Advocates Befriend the Governor and Secure a Victory

Why not start at the top and run a candidate for governor who understands and respects the needs of young children? That's exactly what a group of citizen advocates did in North Carolina when they befriended gubernatorial candidate Jim Hunt and helped him build a platform focused on young children and education in 1992. And then, when Hunt was elected to office, the fruits of their labor were realized.

Smart Start, passed by the state legislature in 1993, is a $20 million pilot project that provides funding and technical assistance to county-level public-private partnerships that design and implement services and programs for all children from birth to age five. In the first wave of the project, 12 partnerships covering 18 counties were funded. Since then, Smart Start has expanded to 81 partnerships in all of North Carolina's 100 counties and is now funded at $260 million.

Smart Start is administered by the North Carolina Partnership for Children, which sets broad statewide goals but provides significant flexibility to the local partnerships in designing and implementing the project according to the unique needs and resources in each area. Local partnerships have boards of directors made up of school superin-

tendents, county health and mental health department heads, teachers, child care providers, parents, librarians, business leaders, and others. A significant amount of collaboration and cooperation is required to reach agreement on funding. Most partnerships dedicate resources to child care subsidies, teacher education and support, health services, and family-support programs.

Having Governor Hunt as the champion for Smart Start was critical. Anytime there was the slightest opposition to the project—from those who thought that children would be harmed by a state-run program to those who worried about government intrusion into family matters—the governor was able to speak eloquently about the importance of early child development, the need for more investments in the early years, and the results realized because of Smart Start. Wherever he was—on a hog farm or at the state capitol—he talked about Smart Start and the benefits for young children.

The early childhood community is delighted by this attention to early care and education, but their job isn't over. For every $10 of state funding, $1 must be raised as either cash or in-kind contributions. Governor Hunt has been highly effective in garnering the support of the busi-

for the Youngest Children in North Carolina

ness community, which has made significant contributions to this program over the years.

Accomplishments

Smart Start realized the following accomplishments:

• *providing preventive health care to children*. More than 297,000 children have received early intervention and preventative health screenings, including vision, dental, and developmental screenings. With such screenings, problems are detected early, and some developmental delays and disabilities are prevented.

• *increasing school readiness.* Smart Start research shows that children who receive the project's services are better prepared when they enter school.

• *serving additional children.* More than 132,000 children have received child care subsidies providing their working parents with affordable child care.

• *building higher quality child care.* Research by the Frank Porter Graham Child Development Center shows that the number of quality child care centers has increased by more than 60 percent.

• *providing parenting and health education resources.* More than 158,000 parents have received parent education resources, often provided in the family home.

• *enhancing local collaboration.* Prior to Smart Start, the school system, child care system, health system, and others operated separately. Because of the local partnership teams, people in these systems are now coming together to work on issues that are important to young children and that cut across their agencies or traditional scope of work.

• *empowering the child care community.* Participating on the local partnership teams has empowered the child care community, which now sees itself as playing on the same field as the school superintendent and other leaders of the community. This empowerment has made the community an even stronger policy advocate. With staff support, each Smart Start partnership soon will be participating in Tuesday for Tots, when partnerships will go to the state capitol and lobby elected officials. The partnerships want to focus attention on important votes for children and remind legislators that the early care and education community is watching.

(continued on p. 58)

Advocates Befriend the Governor (cont'd)

Lessons learned

In its endeavors, Smart Start learned the following lessons:

• It is critically important to have a champion who can articulate the issues clearly and garner the support of a wide group of people. Governor Hunt had the respect of the business community, the faith community, and the education and early childhood communities—key for making Smart Start a success.

• A program can become politicized very quickly, as did Smart Start even though Governor Hunt championed its cause. Accordingly, bipartisan support must be gained early, and legislators need to see that children's issues are the state's issues, regardless of party affiliation.

• It is vital to the success of a project that its leaders have a clear vision and not waver from it.

Based on a January 2001 telephone interview with Geelea Seaford, public information officer for Smart Start.

If you cannot get a majority of members to agree to vote for the amendment, you may decide not to offer the amendment after all. An advocate and the member of Congress must decide the strategy together: whether the amendment should be withdrawn with a statement, whether it should simply be withdrawn, or whether it should be offered as an amendment to the bill when the bill reaches the floor.

After the committee votes on all the amendments, it takes a final vote on whether to report the bill out favorably to the full chamber. A reprinted bill shows additions to the original in italic type and deletions from the original language with strike-throughs. The committee staff writes a report that accompanies the bill, outlining its legislative history, the rationale for the bill itself and for any amendments to it, and a section-by-section analysis.

Step 5: Floor action—Amendments and passage

Now the majority and minority leaders consult on a schedule for the entire chamber to consider the bill. Whenever possible, the more significant and controversial matters are considered under unanimous-consent agreements limiting debate and time on the measure, any amendments thereto, and any debatable motions relating to it. This is done because debate would otherwise be unlimited.

House and Senate rules for floor consideration differ. Once a bill is on the floor before the Senate or House, any member can amend it. Your group may want to support or oppose these amendments. In either case, write a letter stating your position and send copies to each member of the chamber. Be clear about why you support or oppose the specific amendment.

In the House, any member who wants to offer an amendment to a bill on the floor must first file the amendment before the Rules Committee, which then decides whether to allow the amendment to be offered. By contrast, in the Senate a senator may rise to offer an amendment at any time without notice. As a result, advocates may not always know in advance what amendments will be offered on the Senate floor. Theoretically, the amendment must be germane to the subject matter of the bill, but this rule is liberally interpreted.

Sometimes the majority and minority leaders will agree to a limit on the number of amendments that either party may offer on a bill. This usually happens with important bills of broad scope. It is an effort to keep either side from delaying a vote on final passage by indefinitely offering amendments.

Step 6: Conference negotiations

Sometimes, instead of companion bills moving in parallel in the House and Senate, a bill passes one chamber and is sent directly to the other chamber for a vote.

When the House and Senate pass bills for the same program with differing content, the bills must go to a Conference Committee made up of members from both chambers and from the committees with jurisdiction over the bills. The conferees negotiate only matters that differ in the bills passed in the two chambers. Any language that is identical is not subject to conference; language that is similar is. Sometimes one chamber has entire programs and sections that are not part of the other chamber's companion bill. These can be negotiated and either adopted or deleted from the final report, with or without changes. Any matter that is not germane or that is beyond the scope of the differences between the two bills cannot be added at conference time, nor can conferees use the conference to insert new matters into the bill.

Once the conferees end their negotiations, they issue a conference report that both chambers must approve. Here again, advocates may want to take a position in favor of or in opposition to the conference report. If the conference report is not approved, then it is unlikely that Congress will take up that particular bill again that year.

After all amendments have been voted on, but before the final vote on the bill, a member of the House may offer a motion to recommit the bill, together with instructions, to the committee that reported it out. If your group opposes the legislation, find a champion to offer the motion to recommit. This is essentially the last opportunity to generate calls to ask legislators to oppose the bill by voting in favor of the motion to recommit. If the motion to recommit passes, there is no vote on final passage until the revised bill is reported back from the committee.

Step 7: Signing or veto

If both bodies vote in favor of the conference report, the bill is sent to the president (or governor if it is a state bill), who has the option to sign or veto the bill. If signed, the bill is given a public law number and becomes statute. If vetoed, then the bill's proponents must decide if they have enough votes to override the veto.

Implementation: Regulation and guidance

The advocate's role does not end when the legislation is signed into law, for it must still be implemented. Advocates have two primary roles at this stage: helping organizations and the public understand how to implement the new law effectively, and assisting the agency administering the new program or policy to write regulations and guidance to ensure the best outcome is achieved.

Regulations

Regulations are rules promulgated by the executive branch of government, and they have the force of law. These rules help in the administration and enforcement of laws.

Regulations can dramatically affect how a new law is implemented. During the regulatory process, the executive branch can puts its stamp on the new statute. When the executive and legislative braches are not of one mind, it is even more important for advocates to engage in the regulatory process.

Regulatory process

There is a process at the federal level and in state governments for promulgating regulations. In general terms, it involves an agency giving public notice of intent to issue regulations followed by an opportunity for the public to comment on the proposed text or outline of the regulation, and finally the issuance of the final text of the regulation.

Over the last decade, the federal government has given more leeway to states in determining how to implement new federal law. This shift in power is known as devolution. As a result, in some areas such as elementary and secondary education new programs have been created by the legislative branch without accompanying regulations from the executive branch. At the state level, legislation can be very broad and state policymaking culture thus relies much more on regulation.

Advocates should pay equal attention to the regulatory and legislative processes. Working with coalitions that help with the passage of legislation, advocates should be informed about the federal and state regulatory processes and use their grassroots networks to attend and speak at public hearings and submit written comments.

Guidance

It is important for advocates to determine whether the executive branch intends to issue regulations or to provide guidance. Guidance documents do not have the same force as regulations. Like regulation, they are developed by the appropriate agencies and provide information on how to implement a law (as interpreted by the executive branch). Typically, the development of guidance documents does not entail the notice and comment process of regulations, so advocates must make an effort to contact the appropriate agency and try to help shape the final guidance document.

From Legislation to Regulatory Implementation

When President Bush signed the Child Care and Development Block Grant into law in October of 1990, advocates who had worked tirelessly for passage of the legislation did not rest. They immediately came together to promote regulations that would implement the legislation to work for families and children as they had envisioned it would.

First, advocates met to decide their principles for regulations. They next met with administration offices to educate them on important child care issues. They invited the agency staff charged with writing the regulations to visit child care programs so that they could see firsthand the challenges and opportunities of providing child care assistance. When

the Administration published its notice for public comment, the coalition of advocates met and decided on a unified, simple message for their collective response.

When the interim regulations were published, advocates were aghast. The regulations dramatically undercut the states' flexibility to provide high-quality child care with this new funding stream. Advocates worked with the National Conference of State Legislators and the American Public Welfare Association to present a unified front on necessary changes to the regulations and the need to support quality child care programs with the new subsidies. Instead of relying on internal conversations, they took public action. They reached out to

Celebrating and moving forward

After all the hard work is done, it is important for a group to celebrate its efforts. Even if you did not "win," you made a purposeful, serious effort and you should congratulate your advocacy colleagues and yourself with a celebration. If your efforts resulted in positive change, share the good news with others. Make sure everyone in your organization as well as other advocacy allies know what you have accomplished.

It is also important to reflect upon and review your efforts with an eye toward your future goals. What aspects of your strategy were most members of Congress to challenge the Administration's proposals for the regulations. They contacted reporters to tell the story of how the legislation was essentially being rewritten by the regulations. The *New York Times*, the *Washington Post*, *Newsday*, and other major media outlets ran stories on the controversial regulations.

As a result of the public spotlight, a number of the changes proposed by the advocates were made. For example, states were allowed to have higher standards for publicly funded child care and to have some differential rates for quality care.

Accomplishments

The group of advocates succeeded by:

- keeping their coalition together and expanding it to include new players.

- getting their message out in the press to influence public opinion.

- using legislative champions as allies in the regulatory process.

Lessons Learned

The group of advocates learned these lessons from this experience:

- The regulatory process is a critical part of advocacy work.

- The media can have a powerful impact on shaping policy.

- The importance of being vigilant and persistent.

Based on a telephone interview in November 2001 with Helen Blank, Director of Child Care and Development at the Children's Defense Fund.

successful? Did your effort set a precedent for moving a bigger agenda next year? How can you modify your strategies and materials to be effective in a new policy environment? In policy advocacy, as in all types of advocacy, long-term success is gained from learning the lessons of incremental victories.

Endnote

1. Resource used for this section: National Association of State Budget Officers, *Budget processes in the states* (Washington, DC: Author, 1999). Available in hard copy and online at www.nasbo.org.

CHAPTER 4

Other Non-Legislative Opportunities for Making Public Policy

T here are multiple policymaking or policy-influencing opportunities in addition to working with state and federal legislatures. Many boards, commissions, councils, and other groups and officials at the state and local levels have authority to make rules and regulations and in some instances, make laws. Some of them, such as school boards, make decisions about how to spend local tax dollars and other resources. Another way to make laws and policies is through the initiative and referendum process, sometimes referred to as "citizen legislation." Yet another way to make policy is through the judicial process. Below are policymaking arenas that advocates should consider to move their policy agenda forward.

State and local school boards

In addition to the governor, state legislature, and government agencies, there are boards and commissions at the state and local levels that make policy and control public funding decisions. For example, the state board of education (appointed by the governor in most states) creates policies regarding the selection of school reform methods, assessments, teacher licensure requirements, and sometimes textbook selection.

School boards and superintendents

School boards are also important to your efforts. They control a large budget and make policy decisions for the public elementary and secondary schools. Increasingly, they also are the oversight and administrative body for state-funded prekindergarten programs. In addition, many school boards coordinate with other agencies and community organizations to support family literacy, children's mental and physical health, before- and after-school programs, and nutrition programs.

Nationwide, there are roughly 15,000 local school boards, the majority of which are elected by their communities. School board members include parents, business leaders, community leaders, and interested citizens who want a voice in education policy for their local elementary and secondary schools. School boards are an example of the democratic process of decisionmaking. By law, their meetings and hearings must be open to the public (with a few exceptions to protect privacy rights of individuals). Board members debate and vote on policy matters. They do not, however, undertake the daily administration of the school system. That is the role of the superintendent, who is typically hired by the school board.

Many of the matters before a school board concern the use of the budget. Should money be appropriated for after-school programs? If so, what kinds of programs? To what extent should funds be spent on creating full-day kindergarten? Is there a plan for reducing class size, and what will it cost in terms of hiring more teachers and expanding school buildings? Other school board matters involve education reform policy, such as selection of assessment instruments and text books, teacher training in literacy, social promotion, and grade-retention criteria, just to name a few.

The school district superintendent is another potential ally. Superintendents administer the federal, state, and local funds and oversee the implementation in the schools. They also work with other agencies to provide family linkages to health services, after-school care, and adult literacy programs.

Here are some actions to consider:

❖ Find out the schedule for hearings, especially those that deal with setting priorities for the coming year's budget. Prepare materials for the school board members on ways to support early childhood education in the community. Provide linkages between providers and local schools to enhance resource-and-referral services, especially for after-school programs.

❖ If your school district oversees or has a role in a state-funded prekindergarten program, prepare documents on the availability of quality early childhood programs in the community that can help provide prekindergarten education.

❖ Ask the superintendent for a schedule of funded teacher-training offerings, especially Title I. This federal program encourages joint training of early childhood educators and public school teachers with the goal of helping children reach state and local standards, such as reading requirements. Request that the superintendent make these professional development opportunities available to early childhood educators in the community.

❖ Send the superintendent and school board a letter signed by all advocacy partners that addresses policy issues, such as the need to restore recess for children in the early grades or to adjust kindergarten entrance criteria. Make sure the letter has accurate facts about the policies and the impact they have on children and school staff. If possible, include any research or studies that support your position. Make a clear recommendation for what you think the policy should be. Ask the school board to speak to this subject at a board meeting. Invite parents, teachers and teachers' unions, and principals to show support for your position either as co-signers of your letter or with a letter of their own.

Advocacy at the local level can be highly personal. You may know many of the leaders in your community—school board members, leaders of civic organizations, religious organizations, business organizations, and so on. Your advocacy goal may be to affect policy or to address an issue that is relevant only to your program, such as strengthening parent involvement or donating books and computers or volunteer readers.

At the local level

We often hear that "All politics is local"—meaning that policies made at any level have an impact on us and our communities in very concrete ways. Also, it means that policymakers—particularly elected officials—respond to their constituents much more than they do to good ideas that are not visibly connected to those constituents' concerns or voting habits.

Advocates for children have found that starting at the local level is a productive strategy. If the climate or agenda set by the governor and state legislature is not in your favor, you may have more success convincing your mayor and council to dedicate part of the city budget to child care rate increases or compensation, or asking your school board to provide teachers in the early grades with inservice training in child development and effective literacy practices. Then you can move from several local successes to a statewide initiative.

There are many different players at the local level, many of whom have authority over resources and policy that make a difference for young children and families. Some of the government entities that child advocates need to work with are mayors, city councils, and local school boards. Local government officials care about young children and families for different reasons. They want families to move into the cities. They want new businesses that bring jobs and increased spending to the community. Local governments care about quality-of-life issues such as schools and child care availability.

Task Forces and Commissions

Government officials, professional groups, and volunteer organizations may appoint special commissions and task forces. Most task forces include staff, interested citizens, and knowledgeable professionals among their membership. Task forces usually document problems and make recommendations for action. Task forces and commissions can generate consensus on issues and, by soliciting input from experts, introduce new possibilities.[1]

As a member of a task force, you have the opportunity, either as an individual or as a representative of a professional organization, to influence the direction of policymaking from within, rather than outside, the system.[2] Sitting on a task force can be an especially effective way to influence the development or revision of administrative rules and regulations.

Unfortunately, officials sometimes appoint task forces in an attempt to delay real decisionmaking while presenting an image of interest and concern. Other times, to please everyone, a group's recommendations are so watered down that they are meaningless. Even if you are concerned about the nature of the group, it may well be worth joining if your skills and knowledge can help move the issues forward and maintain the group's direction.

Source: Adapted, by permission of the authors, from S. Goffin & J. Lombardi, *Speaking Out: Early Childhood Advocacy* (Washington, DC: NAEYC, 1988), 72–73.

It is important to understand the multiple ways in which different parts of a municipal government impact the lives of young children. The planning and zoning department regulates where child care programs can be located. The recreation department operates child care and after-school programs. The public libraries provide family literacy services. The health department works with schools and early childhood programs to help children receive immunizations and other health care. Even fire departments get involved by visiting schools and teaching children fire prevention and safety.

According to a National League of Cities survey, a significant number of cities are involved in some way in child care or after-school programs.[3] Many provide direct funding for program operations. City officials also often take the lead in advocating or convening groups in support of child care and before- and after-school programs. Some municipalities have a staff person, department, or commission dedicated to these issues.

Here are some actions for advocacy groups to consider:

❖ Take a look at the city's master plan and find out who is in charge of the human services component. Every city has a master plan that largely looks at land use, which is important in terms of setting up public playgrounds, parks and recreation centers, schools, and sidewalks. Find out when this is being reviewed and revised. This plan is also a good source for data about the population and transportation patterns in your city.

❖ Talk to the heads of the parks and recreation, library, housing, and health agencies. They work with families but may not be well informed about or have information for families on how to find quality child care or after-school programs.

❖ For accurate and up-to-date data on the populations in your community, turn to local government as a source of demographic information on age, ethnicity and race, income patterns, business and residential patterns, and other topics. Cities conduct surveys regularly, and this information is a public resource.

Other local boards and groups

The local level affords many opportunities to speak out on behalf of children. A growing number of localities are establishing local planning councils that assess community needs for child care and other family-support services and then collaborate in the delivery and financing of

Californians Support Tobacco Tax for Comprehensive

Counties throughout California are redesigning service systems to provide comprehensive, integrated services for children from before birth to age five. Funding for the effort—approximately $750 million annually—comes from an additional tax on cigarettes and other tobacco products of 50 cents per pack.

A bill allowing for the funding was passed in 1998 as part of a statewide ballot initiative commonly known as Proposition 10, or the California Children and Families First Initiative. Just one year after Proposition 10 passed, California's voters were faced with Proposition 28—a repeal of the tax, which was championed by the tobacco industry. Fortunately, 72 percent of the vote was against repeal, and thus Proposition 10 was not overturned.

The battle was not easily won. The tobacco industry poured tens of millions of dollars into the two campaigns, and after the passage of Proposition 10, multiple lawsuits were filed by the industry that threatened the new law. To counter the opposition, Proposition 10 organizers and supporters worked feverishly to build a broad base of bipartisan support, drawing upon the aid of both traditional (e.g., child care resource-and-referral agencies, local child care planning councils, and early childhood nonprofits) and nontraditional (e.g., the business community, law enforcement, the district attorneys, and organized labor) allies.

The organizers were committed to having a presence in every county throughout the state; consequently, they set up public events with local officials to call attention to the dangers of prenatal smoking, the effects of smoking on youth, and the need for comprehensive, integrated services for the state's youngest children and their families. Events were held in many localities, especially where an analysis of voting trends suggested that the local voters did not hear the original message of Proposition 10.

The media were an important tool. Organizers worked with editorial boards to secure endorsements and increase coverage of the dangers of smoking during pregnancy, the effects of smoking on youth, and the importance of early care and education. Television ads were concentrated in the three major cities: Los Angeles, San Francisco, and San Diego. A communications consultant was hired to focus on outreach to the Latino community through Latino newspapers, radio, and television. An extensive Internet advertising campaign in both Spanish and English

Early Child Development Programs

also called attention to the issues and informed voters.

A campaign for Proposition 10 was established by director/actor Rob Reiner; the campaign was then expanded to encourage voters to say "No on 28." Reiner was primarily responsible for raising the funds to support the effort—some $13.5 million. While that is a lot of money, it is far from the $33 million the tobacco industry spent to defeat the initiative. The campaign had a staff of five, and a handful of consultants, and relied heavily on local child care networks to spread the word. Alliances were formed with the American Heart Association, the American Lung Association, and the American Cancer Society, all of which helped staff the outreach efforts county by county. Fight Crime: Invest In Kids also hired field staff to support the cause.

Accomplishments

The campaigns for Proposition 10 and against Proposition 28 resulted in a number of accomplishments:

• engaging local communities in planning. Each county undertook a countywide planning process to identify its vision for a comprehensive, integrated system for young children and their families. The pro-

cess was led by local Children and Families First Commissions, five- to nine-member bodies that included parents, child care providers, child care advocates, a member of the board of supervisors, and others. Funds now flow to each county to implement its plan.

• increasing services for young children and their families. Already as a result of Proposition 10, more pregnant women receive prenatal care, more children are immunized, more families receive home visiting services, parents of every newborn get a parenting kit, more early literacy programs are available, and more child care providers receive additional training and compensation.

• decreasing smoking. While the majority of the Proposition 10 funding goes directly to the counties to provide services and support for children from before birth to age five and for their families, some of the funds are reserved at the state level for supporting anti-smoking mass media campaigns that target pregnant women and parents of young children. In the first year after Proposition 10 became effective, the state experienced a decrease of 18 percent in cigarette sales.

(continued on p. 72)

Nationwide, smoking is increasing among 18- to 20-year-olds, but smoking in California is down for this same age range. Of course, this decrease in smoking reduces the amount of funding available for counties to carry out their Proposition 10 plans, but it is a positive change for the health and well being of the community.

• increasing public support and understanding of early childhood. Californians are better educated on early childhood issues as a result of the campaigns. An impressive 72 percent of the vote for Proposition 28 was against the repeal of the cigarette tax and for providing comprehensive early care and education services to children.

Lessons learned

The two campaigns yielded several lessons:

• Have a prominent leader spearhead the cause, contributing not only a recognizable name but also significant amounts of time for editorial board meetings, press conferences, special events, and fundraising.

• Enlist bipartisan support.

• Focus on building support at the local level, reaching out to the mayor, city council representatives, sheriff, police chief, labor leaders, and others in the community who are recognizable, trusted leaders.

• Reach out to the education community, bringing in teachers' associations, parent-teacher organizations, and superintendents to highlight the connection between early child development and readiness for school.

Based on a March 2001 telephone interview with Chad Griffin, the former campaign manager for Proposition 10 and "No on Proposition 28."

the recommended programs. Your advocacy for children can take the form of either being a member of these local councils or advising them as an outside advocate.

Many times, officials appoint advisory boards or task forces that help shape policy and program decisions. By becoming members of such a board, individual advocates or representatives from professional groups can share their early childhood perspectives to help inform the group's decisionmaking. Participation on advisory boards provides a direct way to influence decisions that affect children's well-being. At the same time, an advocate can assist other professionals and parents in learning more about early childhood education.

There is also a growing movement in communities to create local child care or other local councils. North Carolina's Smart Start program provides funds to local councils in every county in the state to determine what children and families in the county need, ranging from child care assistance to health and family support services.

Citizen legislation: The initiative and referendum process

Sometimes, citizens take the public policy process into their own hands through the initiative or referendum process.[4] Beginning with the first ballot initiative in Oregon in 1904, advocates have used this process as another opportunity to make public policy. When faced with an unsympathetic state legislature, advocates sometimes turn to the ballot initiative and referendum process as an alternative policymaking vehicle. As in any policymaking effort, advocates need to weigh the political climate and assess their resources to determine whether this is the process that will be most successful to their goals. Twenty-four states have some form of initiative process; forty-nine states have legislative referendum; and twenty-four states have popular referendum. Many counties and cities also give the people the power of the initiative and referendum process. Neither process, however, exists at the federal level.

State laws can be adopted and state constitutions can be amended in many states by the *initiative process*. There are two kinds of initiatives: direct and indirect. In a direct initiative, citizens place constitutional amendments or statutes directly on the ballot for voters to approve or reject. In the indirect initiative process, however, the state legislature plays a role. The people propose amendments or statutes through a petition that is submitted to the state legislature during the legislative session. If the legislation does not adopt the statute or amendment, or the proponents of the initiative oppose the way in which the legislature amends the initiative proposal, the proponents may collect additional signatures and have the proposal submitted to the voters. In some states, the legislature can submit an alternative statute or amendment on the same subject matter as the initiative proposal and the voters must choose between the two versions.

Child Care Achievements in Massachusetts

In 1987, a small group of Boston parents founded Parents United for Child Care (PUCC), because of their concern about the lack of affordable, quality child care and after-school opportunities. Their mission was to create and mobilize a vocal constituency of parents to influence child care policy in their communities and at the state level. PUCC is now some 4,000 members strong and an active voice for parents who are seeking better after-school care for their children.

PUCC works to

• elevate the issue of preschool and school-age child care, helping policymakers in Boston and throughout the state understand parents' concerns about the lack of affordable high-quality child care and after-school opportunities for children;

• build and strengthen parent leaders by providing them with training, leadership development activities, and resources; and

• engage community organizations and carry out statewide advocacy on behalf of parents.

From the start, PUCC has been committed to listening to what parents say they need and want, documenting community needs, and then packaging the information so as to advance public policy. Town hall meetings, public hearings, and other forums have provided effective opportunities to invite policymakers and other community and business leaders to hear directly from parents. PUCC's extensive research of the issues and surveys of parents have allowed them to build support for the issues they raise and solutions they propose.

Accomplishments

PUCC has accomplished the following aims:

• *increasing advocacy skills of parents.* Through its 12-week "Parents Growing, Learning and Leading" course, PUCC has trained more than 150 parent leaders in public speaking, legislative advocacy, and working with the media. At the end of the training, parents complete a project such as giving testimony at a public hearing, planning and implementing a meeting, or writing an editorial. PUCC provides nutritious food, child care, and other supports to the parents who volunteer to spend their Saturdays taking the course.

• *ensuring that parents' voices are heard in early care and education programs.* PUCC also trains parents to influence the early care and edu-

Thanks to Active Parents

cation programs their children attend. The "Building Parent Leadership in Quality Programs" course teaches parents how to be effective advocates and how to design a leadership plan for their child's program. The idea is to build a core group of parents who will be highly engaged in the operation of early care and education programs.

• *conducting surveys of parents regarding their child care needs.* PUCC conducted the first citywide survey of child care in Boston, as well as several statewide parent surveys to document child care needs.

• *Advocating for affordable child care for everyone.* In 1997, PUCC launched the Affordable Child Care for Everyone campaign, which engaged large numbers of parents in community-level advocacy to increase access to high-quality, affordable care. The state legislature did not pass the bill that was proposed as part of this campaign, but many of the bill's components were adopted through the state budget process and state administrative efforts.

• *organizing the Boston School Age Child Care Project.* PUCC created the Boston School Age Child Care Project, now a nearly $1.5 million-a-year entity that offers grants to increase access to after-school care for low-income families. Funded through a mix of public and private sources, the project has provided more than 5,000 affordable slots for children needing after-school care.

• *increasing awareness of the need for after-school programs.* In response to PUCC's work organizing parents and highlighting their challenges in finding after-school programs, Boston launched the 2:00 PM to 6:00 PM Initiative, which is focused on coordinating, enhancing, and improving resources for school-age children.

In an initiative aimed at securing long-term financing for after-school care in Massachusetts, PUCC has spent nearly two years researching sources of funding at the local, state, and federal levels. The campaign and the accompanying legislation—which has been jointly filed in the House and Senate—calls for every community in Massachusetts to receive funding based on the number of children aged 5 through 18 in the community. Funding would be provided annually and could be used for quality and infrastructure development.

(continued on p. 76)

Each state with an initiative process has different rules, but there is a common scheme to them[5]:

❖ Preliminary filing of the proposed initiative with the designated state official;

❖ Review of the initiative for its compliance with statutory requirements prior to its circulation;

❖ Circulation of the petition to obtain the required number of signatures;

❖ Submission of the petition signatures to the state elections official for verification of the signatures;

❖ The placement of the initiative on the ballot and subsequent vote.

The *referendum process* enables citizens to adopt or reject amendments to the constitution or laws proposed by state legislature. There are two kinds of referenda: legislative referenda and popular referenda. A legislative referendum occurs when a state official or agency, state appointed constitution revisions commission, or the state legislature submits constitutional amendments, statutes, or bond issues to the people to approve or reject. The popular referendum process gives the people the right to refer, through petition, specific legislation that the legislature has adopted; voters can then reject or approve that legislation.

Using the courts to make policy

The judicial branch of government also makes public policy through its decisions. Class action lawsuits on behalf of a group of people are a primary judicial process for making policy that affects children. In the education arena, many advocates have helped families as plaintiffs sue their state government for violating the state's constitutional language guaranteeing that the state would provide adequate and equitable public education. More than half of the states have had school finance litigation, and many suits have resulted in court decisions directing states to revise their school funding formulas and other equity issues. As a result, many states have passed new legislation and policies to implement the courts' decisions.

For example, the Ohio Supreme Court, after years of litigation, held that the state must provide more funds for low-income school districts. The implementation was left to the legislature. In New Jersey, the state Supreme Court went further than most school finance decisions. In *Abbott V*, the state Supreme Court ordered the state to provide full-day kindergarten and preschool for all three- and four-year-old children and to implement whole school reform as part of its remedy for the inadequate public education provided to children in low-income urban school districts. At the urging of New Jersey advocates in another round of litigation, the state Supreme Court two years later elaborated on the preschool teacher and other program requirements. In 2001, North Carolina's school finance litigation also resulted in a court order mandating that the state provide prekindergarten programs for children in low-income school districts.

If your organization wishes to advocate through the courts, but it does not have the resources to submit a "friend of the court" brief or to take on litigation directly, there may still be opportunities by working in coalition with others. A coalition can also lobby the legislature to enact legislation that fulfills the goals of a favorable court decision and moves your policy agenda forward.

A Proactive State Agency Brings Change to

Sometimes change comes from advocates *within* the system. The Texas Interagency Council on Early Childhood Intervention (ECI) recognized in the early 1990s that a shift was occurring in special needs policy toward emphasizing the provision of services for children with special needs in the child's "natural environment"—that is, in an environment a child without disabilities would live, learn, and play, such as a family home or a childcare center.

This change was implemented through the State's policy that "Service delivery in community-based settings or the family's home was recognized as the best way to ensure that learning promotes participating in home and community life," making it consistent with the infant and toddler program (Part C) of the Individuals with Disabilities Education Act.[6] This was a major difference from such former standard practices as caring for children with special needs in segregated environments where they did not interact with children without disabilities, or providing physical therapy in a clinic where children were removed from their normal routine.

ECI set out to change practices in the field, beginning with a careful overview of existing policies, services, attitudes, and values. Parent involvement was crucial—so important, in fact, that ECI hired a parent of a child with disabilities as a full-time consultant to ensure that parents were properly represented. Parent advocates also continue to make up the majority of the ECI board, in effect making the ECI a parent-governed state agency.

Working with providers and parents, ECI created new state policies for providing early intervention services to infants and toddlers with special needs, the cornerstone of which was an ambitious three-year plan: Between 1994 and 1997 nearly all programs serving Texan infants and toddlers with special needs switched over to provide all services in natural environments. It wasn't easy, and ECI found that over time some service providers chose to leave the field rather than change their practices. The State's final natural environments policy also reflected that a small number of children with special needs may still receive their care in a segregated

Special Needs Policy and Practice in Texas

environment if their needs cannot be met in any other way.

Accomplishments

ECI has met with success in the following:

• improving care for special needs children. Service delivery in community-based settings or in a family's home has been determined the best way to ensure that learning promotes participation in home and community life. Since 1997, the vast majority of all services for Texan infants and toddlers with special needs—98 percent, in fact—have occurred in such natural environments.

• increasing family involvement and satisfaction with their children's care. Under the natural environments policy, families have received more training on how to facilitate their children's developmental progress within their daily routines. According to a statewide Parent Satisfaction Survey, Texan families feel their children are making progress and that parents are actively involved in planning for their children's care and services.

• improving provider service and practice. Service providers have radically changed their staffing patterns and programs, and have realized that they are now making a much greater impact in the lives of the children and families they serve.

Lessons learned

ECI has learned the following lessons:

• Reach out to stakeholders for their input. Parents and providers become invested in change when they are given a chance to be involved.

• Provide training and guidance for both parents and providers in order to effect system-wide change. They need instruction and assistance when adjusting to care in natural environments.

• Allow time for programs to make changes. Progress isn't instantaneous; it takes incremental change to alter attitudes and practices.

• Continue to monitor programs to ensure that they are up-to-date with the latest policies.

_____

Based on a July 2001 interview with Christy Dees, ECI Family Services and Policy Specialist.

Endnotes

1. S.R. Bing, & D.W. Richart, *Fairness is a kid's game: A background paper for child advocates* (Indianapolis: Lilly Endowment, 1987).

2. S. Kilmer, "Early childhood specialists as policymakers," *Education and Urban Society* 12 (1980): 241–51.

3. National League of Cities, *New directions for cities, families and children: Child care systems* (Washington, DC: Author, 1997), 5.

4. To learn more about the initiative and referendum process, and follow activities in your state, contact the Initiative and Referendum Institute at 202-429-5539. They are also available online at www.iandrinstitute.org.

5. M.D. Waters, Testimony presented to the California Commission on the Initiative Process, 18 December 2000.

6. C. Dees, Personal communication, 10 July 2001.

CHAPTER 5

The Advocate's Toolbox

Advocates use a variety of tools to inform and persuade others. The materials should be developed and tailored to different audiences. For example, what should parents know about the full cost of quality child care? What does a public policymaker need to know and what actions are needed from him or her to support good early literacy programs? There are a variety of tools for advocates to use, from issue briefs to talking points and even model legislation.

Preparing advocacy materials before you meet with policymakers or other decisionmakers is important. For one thing, it helps you refine your message and the actions you want taken in support of your agenda. Second, it allows you to be more responsive and credible when a legislator or school board member says, for example, "Please send me some information on that." Going into meetings or being able to immediately follow up on a phone call with the desired information is more professional and, ultimately, more effective than having to ask someone to wait. Be aware, however, that you may need to modify your materials into talking points or other more specific issue briefs as the policy process moves forward.

The purpose of the materials is twofold: to describe the problem and the issue and to make the case for adoption of a particular public policy or change. If you prepare only a set of facts, you will be asked what response you are seeking to them. Remember that legislative staff want to know what you want them to do. If you do not tell them exactly what you are seeking, staff may choose to define it very differently than you would have wanted.

Mobilizing a grassroots network

If anything indicates the greatest change in advocacy, it is the growth of grassroots advocacy at every level. Grassroots advocates are people in the community—not professional advocates—who make their voices heard by elected policymakers around issues of common concern. At times, thousands of grassroots activists have been mobilized by a single alert.

The heart of an advocacy strategy is the mobilization of a network of grassroots activists to contact their elected officials. Legislators and other elected officials are most likely to respond favorably to requests from their constituents. The most powerful tool used to mobilize activists is an action alert.

Important Advocacy Materials

• *Briefing papers.* Each briefing paper should address only one topic at a time. It should describe the problem, focus on the issue, propose the policy you want, and, if possible, give examples of how the policy is working positively for children in other communities or states.

• *Talking points.* Talking points are what they sound like: a few sentences, standing alone, that get your point across quickly. In essence, they are soundbites telling why you support or oppose a particular policy or decision. Advocates should be familiar with talking points, using them in meetings and interjecting them into letters, editorials, and other materials.

• *Key facts.* Sometimes advocates forget that the public, policymakers, and other decisionmakers may not know the basic facts of the issue. What is familiar information to you may be unknown to your audience. Prepare a one- or two-sided page of key facts. Always make sure that your statistics and facts are accurate; you will lose credibility if your facts do not stand up to scrutiny.

Regular updates

When an action alert goes out across the network, the average advocate should not have to spend more than 15 minutes in response. This is possible only when the entire network is comfortable with the issues. Regular updates are critical. Legislative, regulatory, or other advocacy developments can be provided by e-mail, in monthly newsletter columns, or at regular meetings. New legislation and its progress through the legislative process should be addressed. To distinguish them from action alerts, updates should be clearly marked as such and should note "no action requested at this time."

Action alerts

Action alerts are requests for immediate action, not information or news. (See "Sample Action Alert" on p. 84.) A leader's job is to prepare the network and let the advocates know what to cover and when to make contact. Beforehand, make sure you have provided the tools they need, such as talking points, fact sheets, or a sample written or oral message.

In the alert, provide the why, what, who, and when. Start with a few sentences about the purpose of the action and why action must be taken. Then state what action is needed—e-mails, letters, faxes, or phone calls—and when. Make it clear who needs to be contacted, for example advocates' own elected officials, those on a particular committee, or both. Indicate whether there are specific targets for calls or faxes, or that your network should contacted each and every legislator. The most effective alerts include a sample letter or phone script. Remember that the network is made up of volunteers, so anything that can make their contact with a legislator or other decisionmaker easy, clear, and brief is going to be more efficient and effective.

Alert trees

Not everyone has e-mail, and some who do don't always check it regularly. Many advocates need to be alerted through telephone and fax trees. These work like a chain letter: A designated recipient of the action alert starts the process by calling the key contacts and notifying them of the alert. Then the second level of alert recipients makes subsequent calls. Ideally, legislators receive dozens of calls as a result.

A Sample Action Alert

NAEYC Alert April 2, 2001
CALL CONGRESS NOW!

Congress will take up the budget resolution tonight. **Call your senators immediately. All senators must be called.** If you cannot call today, please call tomorrow.

The Capitol switchboard (202-224-3121) connects you to any office.

If the switchboard is busy, go to www.naeyc.org. Click on "Children's Champions" and then on "Action Center." By entering your zip code, you can get the names and phone numbers of your senators. After your phone call or fax, please send a backup e-mail to your senators, using the same Action Center at NAEYC's Website.

Background

The president's detailed budget has not been released, yet the Senate is moving forward on the budget resolution. The president's budget outline of February 28 would redirect $200 million of Child Care and Development Block Grant (CCDBG) funds and says nothing about Head Start funding levels. In addition, *The New York Times* reports that the president's budget will eliminate the Early Learning Opportunities Act (now funded at $20 million)

and shift the funds to early literacy. We believe all of these programs should be funded so that the needs of children and families can be met without making trade-offs between them.

Sample message

I believe no child should be left behind. That is why it is critical that the Senate vote for the following amendments, which will invest in quality early childhood education so that all children will be ready for school and ready to read.

(1) Vote YES on the Harkin "Leave No Child Behind" amendment, which would increase investments in Head Start and the Early Learning Opportunities Act so that young children have quality early learning programs.

(2) Vote YES on the Dodd amendment to increase mandatory spending for the CCDBG so that children will have safe care and parents can go to work. Now, only 12% of eligible children are receiving assistance.

(3) Vote YES on any amendment to make the Dependent Care Tax Credit and Child Tax Credit refundable and YES on any amendment that would put additional new dollars into early childhood education.

Lobby days

Another effective advocacy tool is flooding elected officials with calls, visits, or faxes on a chosen day. For example, your network may call or visit a policymaker with a specific message on a designated Lobby Day or Call-in Day. The point is to create a large volume of voices speaking in unison.

Tips for communicating with legislators

You don't have to be an expert on the issue to communicate well. In deciding which method to use, first be clear about your goals. In all communications with different federal, state, or local policymakers, be strategic and consistent. Choose your form of communication on the basis of desired outcome.

Here are some guidelines for getting your message across:

❖ discuss one subject only

❖ be specific about the action you want taken by the policymaker

❖ show how the legislation or policy will have an impact on children or on educators working with children

❖ be accurate with your facts

❖ personalize, if possible, your communication with your own experience or with anecdotes from your community (that you can document later if need be)

❖ identify your affiliation if pertinent

The various means of communication

Advocates can use a number of methods for communicating with policymakers at every level.

Phone calls

Phone calls, especially en masse, are an effective means of communicating a position or request when timing is critical and a policymaker is about to cast a vote. A telephone tree consisting of many individuals is the most useful organizing tool for getting large numbers of people to call at the same time. A few leaders activate the tree by alerting other advocates to call on the given subject with a certain message: Vote yes or no, as the case may be. The leaders of the tree are responsible for providing the message to use in the calls. The following tips for calling policymakers are useful:

❖ Know whom to call. If the bill you are interested in is in committee, call the chairman of the committee even if your representative does not sit on the committee.

❖ Specify the issue and ask to speak to the aide who handles that issue. Often the aide who handles budget and appropriations is different from the one handling children's and education issues.

❖ If the aide is not available, ask to leave your name, phone number, and a brief message. Remember to get the name of the aide who will receive your message so you can follow up on your phone call.

❖ Be prepared to state your position and the reasons you support or oppose the legislation in no more than three sentences. Ask for the policymaker's position on the legislation.

❖ Tell the aide you would like a message left for the policymaker, and have the aide communicate the position you want the policymaker to take.

❖ You can request a written response to your phone call.

E-mails, letters, and faxes

In this Internet age, advocates increasingly use e-mail to communicate information to their networks and to write to policymakers. But while e-mail is a rapid way to reach the grassroots, it often is not the fastest way to reach policymakers. Surveys of congressional offices show that e-mails sent to the main office address are read sometimes no more than once a week. Usually the person assigned to read the e-mails is a junior staffer who is reading literally hundreds, if not thousands, of e-mails over a brief period of time. However, it is always a good idea to back up phone calls and faxes with an e-mail, if possible.

Letters are effective only if the situation is not urgent. Policymakers at every level receive a lot of mail, and advocate's letters may not be read for some time.

Faxes are another way to indicate, in a very direct way, the level of support or opposition to an upcoming vote. Faxes work best if a large number of your grassroots activists each send one on the same day or, preferably, all on one morning or afternoon. However, as with an e-mail or a letter, you may not receive a response for some time.

❖ Clearly state the purpose of a letter, fax, or e-mail in the first paragraph. Whether in support or opposition, the communication should specify the legislation or regulation, and state your position.

❖ Provide a rationale. You must give a policymaker reasons to agree with your position. Use your personal experience and, if they are available, research reports and studies. (Check out the NAEYC Website for national research on children, child care, and education.)

❖ Be brief. Policymakers receive literally thousands of pieces of mail each week, so keep your letter to one page if you want it to be read. Each letter should address a single issue. If there is more than one issue, write separate letters for each.

❖ Identify yourself. State whether you are a teacher, parent, director, principal, community leader—whatever. If you are a constituent of the legislator, make sure you identify yourself as a resident of the district or state.

Visits

Face-to-face meetings are ideal in educating a policymaker and his or her staff. Try to visit in groups of a size small enough to allow for discussion. Always schedule the visit in advance, and follow up with a thank-you letter and any requested written materials.

❖ Have a strategic reason for the meeting. Before you call to schedule a meeting, be clear about its purpose. Advocates have different reasons for meetings: setting forth a position on a piece of legislation or a regulation, recruiting a sponsor for a piece of legislation, or generally introducing important issues.

Getting the Right Connection

You can reach the offices of your representative and senators directly or through the U.S. Capitol switchboard at any time on any day. Call (202) 224-3121 and ask to be connected to the office.

Find your governor's, state legislator's, or agency's address and phone number through the World Wide Web. Many policymakers and agencies have their own Websites. To find those of state legislatures and individual legislators, check out the National Conference of State Legislators site at www.ncsl.org. The National Governors' Association lists all of the governors' sites at www.nga.org. You can also be linked to the Websites of the different state agencies through the governor's Website.

Calling a Virtual Strike on Behalf of New Hampshire's Children

How do you get real media attention and at the same time organize your state to do something good for children? In New Hampshire, several committee members of Invest in Kids organized a "virtual strike"—in lieu of an actual walkout—by child care workers to call attention to the lack of available, affordable, quality child care in the state.

The aim of the strike was to find ways in which parents and the business and legislative communities could form partnerships to solve their mutual child care crisis. The strike, with support from Children and Family Services of New Hampshire, was called for January 21–26, 2001. Thousands of parents, child care providers, business leaders, and concerned community members across New Hampshire participated. More than 150 organizations, including the New Hampshire Chapter of the American Academy of Pediatrics, endorsed the strike.

Planning for the strike, an effort that required intense grassroots involvement, began in November 1999. The core group of organizers numbered about 12, with one person focusing on the effort for three days a week. A kickoff rally was held in October 2000, and attended by several hundred people, including legislators and a number of business leaders.

Each day of the weeklong virtual strike featured a different event.

• **Monday—Parents' Day.** Child care providers talked with parents about available, accessible, quality child care. The parents were given buttons that said, "This Worker Made Possible by Quality Child Care." Parents were encouraged to wear their buttons to work to demonstrate the fact that child care is a critical issue for their employees.

• **Tuesday—Business Day.** Business leaders throughout the state were invited to visit a local child care center to gain a better understanding of what the children of their employees do during the day and to appreciate the importance of quality child care. In addition, employers were given a list of ideas about what they might do to address the child care crisis.

• **Wednesday—Legislators' Day.** State legislators were invited to visit child care centers and shadow employees at their jobs. The hope was to get at least a dozen legislators to spend two to three hours in a center to learn about the importance of quality child care for all children. Sample letters were available for child care staff and parents to sign and mail to the state legislature, asking for increased reimbursement for their services, increased eligibility for child care subsidies, and access to health insurance by child care workers.

- **Thursday—Child Care Center Personnel Day.** The focus of this day was on helping child care center personnel recognize how important they are, both in terms of providing high-quality care to children and with regard to speaking out on behalf of the children they serve. Center personnel were encouraged to join early childhood organizations as a way to make their voices heard.

- **Friday—Children's Day.** This day featured a wrap-up of the week and celebrated accomplishments.

The organizers of the virtual strike aimed to highlight the child care crisis not only in New Hampshire but also across the country. Discussions are now under way in at least two other states (Vermont and Maine) to organize their own virtual strike. Further, organizers hope that, beyond raising public awareness about the child care crisis, the strike will spur legislators to take action to address some of the most pressing problems (e.g., passing legislation that would provide health care insurance to child care workers).

Accomplishments

Through its virtual strike, Invest in Kids and its partners accomplished the following:

- *increasing public awareness of child care issues.* Several hundred people attended the October pre-strike rally, and even more than that are now on an e-mail listserve and receive at least weekly updates on child care issues. The listserve helps people feel connected and ensures that they have an opportunity to receive information and provide input.

- *invigorating the child care community.* Child care workers, who did nearly all of the planning for the virtual strike, were invigorated and empowered by their involvement. This excitement led to organizing a Child Care Budget Watch in which several center directors, college faculty, and students decided that they would sit in on all of the state legislature's discussions about child care budget issues. They make reports of the meetings available by e-mail to the listserve, thereby ensuring that the child care community has the latest information about all policy and financial discussions. This ensures better responses to plans that might jeopardize child care resources.

- *increasing involvement of the business community.* Efforts to engage representatives of the business community in the virtual strike appear to have been successful.

(coninued on p. 90)

Calling a Virtual Strike on Behalf of New Hampshire's Children (cont'd)

Businesses became involved in the October rally and the virtual strike, and at least one business has opened an on-site child care center since then.

Lessons learned

The virtual strike taught Invest in Kids several lessons:

• Find a specific issue and a particular proposal that people can organize around.

• Adding partners to an e-mail listserve increases awareness and mobilizes more voices for action. But it is still important to have some initial telephone contact with people so that they feel a part of the process.

• Organizing a very public event like a virtual strike takes a lot of work. Make sure that you have the numbers to carry out the work or that you are willing to accept the fact that not everything suggested will be accomplished.

• At the beginning of the process, lay out a plan with a timeline so that you can keep the effort focused and on track.

Based on a December 2000 telephone interview with Jack Lightfoot, child advocate for Child and Family Services of New Hampshire.

❖ Make the appointment in advance with the right people. Always call to set up an appointment. Ask to speak with the legislator's scheduler. Explain the purpose of the meeting, and let the scheduler know who from the legislator's staff should attend (those whose responsibilities are child care, appropriations and budget, or K–12 education, for example). Let the scheduler know the name of each advocate who will be attending the meeting, as well as his or her title or position. If you live in the legislator's district, make sure you tell that to the scheduler.

❖ Be prompt, be patient, and be flexible. Advocates should be on time for meetings. Most policymakers have very tight schedules. You may have to wait for them, but they should not wait for you. If a meeting is interrupted or if a different staff member than the one you requested is there, be flexible.

❖ Have your materials ready. Whenever possible, bring materials that support your position. Brief information sheets and talking points are most effective. Be sure that your position is stated clearly in the first paragraph. Be ready to discuss examples that support your position.

❖ Ask for a commitment. Too often, advocates leave meetings believing that they have won support. Policymakers often use noncommittal phrases like "That is very important," "That's very interesting," or "I agree that this is a critical issue." Make sure that you ask for a commitment: *How* will the legislator vote on the legislation? Will he or she sponsor the bill you requested? Will the language you proposed be included in the final version of the bill?

❖ Follow up. If you did not have written materials for the policymaker at your meeting, or if you need to address some of the policymaker's questions, follow up immediately with the information. Always send a letter expressing your gratitude to the policymaker for meeting with you, and repeat your position. If a commitment was made, restate it in the letter.

Testimony

Public written testimony submitted to a legislative or other type committee, school board, local council, or Congress can be offered voluntarily to become part of the record, but check the rules on uninvited testimony before you begin. If you are seeking the opportunity to orally testify, you may need to make the request in writing and explain why your perspective should be heard. If you are speaking on behalf of a coalition or organization, be sure to make note of that. Be specific about the actions you think policymakers should take on the issue.

This toolbox is not static. As information changes advocates need to keep their materials up-to-date and tailored to new needs and changing audiences. Being prepared will help you make your case in a timely and effective manner.

CHAPTER 6

Getting Your Message Out

N ot everything advocates do is a news story. Before asking a
reporter to cover something, advocates should ask themselves,
"Is it news?" A conference is not necessarily news. Usually, only an
event that calls for action, such as a rally in front of the city council
building, is news. A survey of early childhood staff that reports on low
salaries, increasing turnover rates, and the impact on both young children and the local economy can be a news story. Accreditation of a
community child care center is newsworthy in local papers, but probably is
not a front-page story.

Using the media effectively

The media are critical to moving an agenda. The question you must
pose is "Are we 'committing' news?" Are you making news or simply
telling an interesting story? What would make your point newsworthy?
If your goal is to inform and educate the public about an issue, should
you consider writing a letter to the editor or creating a public service
announcement to be aired on the radio?

Here are ten dos and don'ts to remember in working with the media[1]:

1. Do limit yourself to three points, but be prepared to make them
   clearly and cogently.

2. Do back up your assertions with credible data from recognized sources.

3. Do speak from personal experience if it's relevant.

4. Do answer every question, but come back to your three points.

5. Do use quotable, strong phrases.

6. Don't go overboard with exaggerated language that makes you sound like an extremist.

7. Don't chat or gossip with reporters; what you say could be on the record.

8. Don't try to get reporters' attention when you don't have anything newsworthy to give them.

9. Don't drone on; keep your replies crisp and to the point.

10. Don't drop a press contact after one interview; build a relationship over time.

Tools

Media list. You should compile a thorough list of media in your region, including local newspaper, radio, and television reporters, columnists, and talk show hosts. At a minimum, learn the name, work phone number, fax number, and e-mail address of the reporters who cover children, family, and education issues. Also know which reporters are interested in politics and business and workplace issues.

Media kit. A media kit contains basic information about an organization or coalition, a fact sheet on the issues, the names of spokespeople, any positive press clippings about your organization or the issue, and a cover memo tailored to the particular media you are contacting.

Responding to reporters

As your coalition or organization becomes more vocal and known, reporters are likely to call spokespeople or leaders for information or for a position. When responding to a call, remember that reporters are under a strict deadline and have been assigned to write a certain story by their editor. You cannot change the story, but you can offer facts to make it more accurate or more interesting.

Whenever an advocate gets a call, he or she should always ask:

❖ the name of the publication.

❖ the deadline for filing the story.

❖ whether he or she will be quoted, and if so, ask the reporter to read back the quote to ensure its accuracy.

Remember, there is really no such thing as "off the record." You can provide background material and ask that you not be quoted or not have your remarks attributed to you or the organization. However, if you know the reporter or are developing a relationship with a reporter this request may hamper his or her willingness to work with you again. Therefore, think carefully about whether you need to speak off the record at all.

Speaking out: Press releases

A press release normally should be no longer than one page. It can be an announcement or a commentary. It should state up front what is of interest to the media. The contact for follow-up information should be clear, with phone and e-mail information provided. It should include a quote from the organization's executive director that can be used in the story or that draws the reporter to call and follow up.

The embargo. If you are planning to release a report, a survey, or a poll, get the material to the media in advance so that reporters can pull together the background of the story beforehand. Clearly mark on the cover and in your cover letter that the materials are "EMBARGOED" until the date and time they are slated for public release. Generally, reporters are used to embargoed material and will respect your request.

Misquotes, errors, and corrections. If you are misquoted or you think facts are stated incorrectly, you may want to ask for a correction. Carefully consider whether to make this request, because in doing so you are essentially criticizing the reporter for his or her work. If you desire an ongoing relationship with the reporter (e.g., the assigned education or political reporter for the local paper or radio station), you may decide that asking for a correction is not worth the potential loss of your relationship. As in all things, be strategic and decide how great the error really is. Everyone gets misquoted, but were you misquoted in a way that substantially changes your organization's position? If the error is serious, politely request that a correction be posted in another story.

Public service announcements. Use public service announcements (PSAs) to educate and influence the public. Usually, a PSA is an audio- or videotape sent to a television or radio station in ready-to-air condition. Stations have guidelines for placing PSAs, so contact them to make sure that your materials and your purpose fall within the guidelines.

For more information, contact Alan Simpson at NAEYC
202-328-2605 or asimpson@naeyc.org

NAEYC Issues New Standards for Early Childhood Teacher Preparation
A Key Step to Raising Quality of Early Childhood Education Programs

WASHINGTON, DC, October 29, 2001—Responding to the growing need for better qualified teachers of children from birth through age eight, the National Association for the Education of Young Children (NAEYC) has released revised standards for the college and university programs that prepare early childhood teachers.

"High-quality early education programs give young children a foundation for success in school and beyond, but unfortunately there aren't enough high-quality programs available. A crucial step in raising the quality of programs for all young children is improving the preparation of early childhood teachers," said Mark Ginsberg, Ph.D., Executive Director of the National Association for the Education of Young Children.

The revised Standards for Early Childhood Professional Preparation are based on extensive research in early childhood development and learning, and were reviewed by dozens of early education experts and organizations. The revised standards include:

- Greater focus on academic content, cultural and linguistic diversity, and young children with special needs;
- Stronger emphasis on practical experience and preparation; and
- Increased concentration on the outcomes of teacher preparation programs and the effect they will have on young children's learning.

As one of the specialty professional associations working with the National Council for the Accreditation of Teacher Education (NCATE), NAEYC prepared these standards as a guide for higher education institutions that prepare future early childhood teachers. The programs must document how they comply with the standards in order to earn approval from NAEYC—and move toward accreditation from NCATE.

NAEYC's revision of the standards is part of a growing dialogue in the early childhood education field about the importance of teacher preparation. The National Research Council's recent report, *Eager to Learn: Educating Our Preschoolers*, called for all early childhood teachers to have a bachelor's degree with a specialty in early childhood. In addition, a recent national survey of early childhood teacher preparation programs at colleges and universities warned that those programs are unprepared for the growing national and state demand for better-trained teachers. That study, from the National Center for Early Development and Learning at the University of North Carolina (Chapel Hill) said the institutions are also ill-equipped to prepare teacher candidates for the challenges of the field, including working with infants, young children with disabilities, and children from diverse linguistic and cultural backgrounds.

The focus on teacher preparation is also an essential part of NAEYC's comprehensive approach to improving the quality of early childhood education. The other parts include raising standards for early childhood programs (through NAEYC accreditation), improving the practices of teachers, and enhancing approaches to early childhood curriculum content and assessment. "If our society really wants to help all young children grow and learn, we need to make greater commitments in several areas. Improving the preparation of new teachers is an important step in the right direction," said Ginsberg.

* * *

The National Association for the Education of Young Children is the largest organization of early childhood educators and others committed to improving the quality of early education programs for children birth through age eight.

It is best to get professional help in producing a PSA. Consult an advertising firm or a public-relations firm, for example. The cost of producing a PSA depends on its length and whether you choose television or radio. Most PSAs are 15, 30, or 60 seconds long. Because cost is a factor, make sure the tape fits the station's format. Many PSAs are "live copy": that is, you provide the script and a radio announcer reads the message.

Opinion-editorials (op-eds) and letters to the editor. Before advocates write, they should ask the newspaper for its guidelines for submitting an op-ed or letter to the editor. Many have word or space limits. Also ask for the name of a contact, a fax number, or an e-mail address so your submission goes to a specific person. Sometimes the messenger is as important as the message. You may want to have an op-ed piece or letter submitted by someone else in your community, such as a well-known doctor, school superintendent, religious leader, or law enforcement official.

The distinguishing features of an op-ed is a clear and strong point of view. Take a strong position on a contentious issue, and state your topic and viewpoint at the beginning of your article. Support your position with compelling facts and data. Your article should conclude with a call to action or a clear restatement of your main point.

Letters to the editor build awareness of your organization and its position on an issue. Typically, letters respond to articles or editorials that have appeared in the paper in the previous few days. Frame your argument as you would in an op-ed piece.

Print ads. Print advertising is another valuable medium for reaching people. Start by looking at effective ads on social issues, such as antismoking and environmental campaigns. What works about them? How do they catch your interest? How do they catch the interest of others who may not have a personal stake in the topic? You will notice that the key to a good print ad is a strong visual image and a crisp headline or message, which work together to grab readers' attention. You can include more information, but if your image and headline don't "hook" the readers, they won't read any further.

Do not say too much. Most readers retain one or two messages from an ad, at best. Leave room for lots of empty space, rather than crowd the ad with printed words. Let the pictures speak.

Print ads are extremely expensive, sometimes as much as $40,000 for half a page of a national newspaper. Local newspapers (with the exception

Advocates in Washington State

Getting a story about child care out and aired is now easier in the state of Washington, thanks to the Washington News Service. In 1999 the Children's Alliance mobilized a group of people from nonprofit organizations involved in child care, the environment, affordable housing, and other services. Recognizing that the media are vital to effective advocacy and that radio in particular usually does not cover stories about these issues, the various organizations committed to supporting the development of a news service. With the help of Creative Communications, an Idaho-based consulting firm with experience in developing news services for nonprofits, the Washington News Service was launched. The service has been a highly effective tool for disseminating ready-to-use information on social policy issues to Washington state radio stations.

The Washington News Service feeds radio stations with brief news scripts and recorded soundbites. The scripts are one to two paragraphs long and are carefully written to conform to news standards.

The soundbites are recorded by a spokesperson and are stored on a playback device. The scripts are then sent by broadcast fax to approximately 60 radio stations. When a station wants to run a story provided by the service, the station calls a toll-free telephone number and records the soundbite for playback on the air. During the actual broadcast, the broadcaster simply reads the script and plays the soundbite.

Approximately 30 nonprofit organizations are participating in the service. Each organization pays a participation fee of $2,000 per year that covers the consulting costs for Creative Communications. The Ford Foundation matches all local contributions, thus doubling the work that can be done. General administrative costs of the Washington News Service are covered by the Children's Alliance.

Accomplishments

Among the accomplishments of the Children's Alliance media effort are the following:

of major city papers like *Washington Post, New York Times, Chicago Tribune,* and so on) are less expensive. Typically, the fee is lower if the ad is placed during the week rather than on the weekend. Therefore, carefully select the timing and placement of the ad.

Form Their Own News Service

• **producing and distributing stories.** In the first 18 months of service, 316 stories were produced and were aired a total of 4,000 times on radio stations in markets such as Spokane, Wenatchee, Bellingham, and Centralia.

• **reaching outside the metropolitan market.** The news service has aired stories in smaller market areas that traditionally would not have picked up the stories.

• **perpetuating common themes.** Early in the history of the news service, the Children's Alliance facilitated a conversation with the participating agencies to identify common themes that cut across the mission and goals of the different organizations. Each script and soundbite is designed to reinforce one or more of these themes.

• **increasing the diversity of stories aired.** As the organizations involved become more skilled and savvy media users, they increase the diversity of the stories aired. For example, the service has produced stories about topics such as pay increases for early childhood educators, grants for after-school activities, and state training requirements.

Lessons learned

The Children's Alliance learned the following lessons from its advocacy efforts:

• Make an investment of time up front to work with participating organizations to help them develop common themes. People need to be trained to think beyond the content of their organization's message, to tie it to an overarching theme that will be repeated time and again.

• Help organizations understand how they can get the most out of the service, especially smaller organizations and those without previous media experience. All organizations need to know how to effectively identify and shape a story so that it will appeal to radio stations across the state.

Based on a December 2000 telephone interview with Jon Gould, project coordinator.

Endnote

1. V. Witt, *Getting your message out: Public information and media relations training*, presentation at the 2000 NAEYC Leadership Conference, 5 June 2000 (San Francisco, CA).

Public Engagement

Special events can increase public awareness of early childhood issues. A variety of engagement events can educate the public and make them sympathetic to your issues. The information advocates provide will hopefully spur greater interest and more active support of the issues among the general public. Although public events can be planned throughout the year, they are especially appropriate for the Week of the Young Child. This event, usually celebrated in April, is sponsored by NAEYC. Its purpose is to raise people's awareness of the needs of young children and their families.

Conferences, workshops, and seminars build awareness of specific issues and help participants plan strategies for action.

Celebrations, festivals, or fairs bring children, parents, and educators together for a good time. They can focus attention on an issue such as appropriate early education practices.

Open houses and tours of early childhood programs enable parents and the general public to become better informed about such programs.

Shopping mall activities and exhibits can increase your group's visibility as well as public sensitivity to early childhood issues.

A speakers' bureau can be a resource for informing community groups about important early child-

hood issues. Speakers' bureaus both arrange for speakers to give talks on a variety of topics and help connect them with interested groups. If possible, speakers should represent a wide range of child- and family-related professions: psychologists, health workers, and children's librarians, for example. This increases constituency support for your issues.

All of these events take planning, effort, and cooperation. Identify your goals, select the kind of event most likely to achieve those goals, and obtain the necessary resources (sites, volunteers, and financial support). Evaluate the event afterward, so that when you plan the next one, you learn from your experiences.

Every community has civic, church, labor, political, and special-interest groups, such as Junior League, Rotary Club, Chamber of Commerce, Parent-teacher associations, Knights of Columbus, unions, and many more. With the growing attention to children's issues, many of these groups are interested in hearing local experts and visiting early childhood programs.

With many public engagement activities, it is important to "paint a picture" that will arouse the interest and support of your audience. Avoid professional jargon and make your point simple.

Source: Reprinted, by permission of the authors, from S. Goffin & J. Lombardi, *Speaking Out: Early Childhood Advocacy* (Washington, DC: NAEYC, 1988), 79–80.

CHAPTER 7

Nonprofit Organizations and Lobbying, Political Activity, and Voter Education

S ection 501(c)(3) in the Internal Revenue Code defines a tax-exempt, nonprofit charitable organization and delineates permissible and prohibited lobbying and political activities (see Appendix D). For example, the National Association for the Education of Young Children is a 501(c)(3) organization. In return for granting exemption from certain federal taxes, the government imposes limitations on the organization's lobbying, political, and voter education activities. These limitations give ample room for organizations to lobby and to engage in voter education, but are more restrictive on political activities. As long as an organization is cognizant of these limitations, keeps records of its activities, and files the necessary forms, there should be no hesitation to advocate on behalf of the needs of young children and families.

Note: The information provided in this chapter does not represent legal advice or representation. If you or your organization intend to engage in lobbying, political activity, or voter education, you should consult the relevant federal and state statutes, regulations, and rulings. This chapter deals only with limitations on 501(c)(3) organizations. If you are acting on behalf of some other type of organization, please check all relevant laws, rules, and regulations. This chapter also does not deal with activities conducted by individuals on their personal behalf.

Lobbying activity

Many nonprofit organizations erroneously assume that they cannot engage in lobbying. Lobbying is a permissible activity—within certain limits. Section 501(c)(3) of the Internal Revenue Code states that a tax exempt charitable organization cannot spend a "substantial part of [its] ...activities carrying on propaganda, or otherwise attempting to influence legislation (except as otherwise provided . . .)".[1] The Internal Revenue Service determines the allowable lobbying activities for a 501(c)(3) organization in one of two ways. An organization can register ("elect") under section 501(h) of the Internal Revenue Code to use a different reporting and expenditure test for lobbying and grassroots activities. If the organization does not file under 501(h), it will automatically have to meet the "substantial" test (described below).

What constitutes lobbying?

For organizations that do not register under section 501(h), lobbying includes attempts to influence legislation, such as urging the adoption or rejection of a bill or amendment, contacting members of a legislative body about legislation, or urging the public or members of the organization to contact legislators. Lobbying also includes preparing positions on legislative measures, including positions formulated on legislation and research, and communicating information about the positions taken.

Legislation is defined as action by Congress, state legislatures, local councils, and similar governing bodies; foreign laws; and public action such as ballot initiatives, constitutional amendments, and referenda. The law is not clear whether legislation includes action by executive, administrative, or judicial branches, but the IRS may interpret attempts to influence such action as lobbying.

Section 501(h) gives clearer guidance to what constitutes lobbying. Under 501(h), there are two kinds of lobbying: direct and grassroots. *Direct lobbying* is when the purpose of the activity is to influence legislation with a member/staff of a legislative body or a nonlegislative government official/employee who participates in developing legislation, but only if the activity refers to and reflects a view on a specific legislative proposal that the organization supports or opposes. Direct lobbying includes communications "directly encouraging" organization members to engage in direct lobbying. Administrative activities, such as trying to influence rulemaking or enforcement by a government agency, do not constitute direct lobbying.

For section 501(h) electors, legislation includes the introduction, amendment, enactment, and repeal of bills, resolutions, or acts of Congress, state legislatures, and local councils. It also includes ballot initiatives, constitutional amendments, and referenda. It does not include actions by administrative or judicial bodies. Contacts with such bodies are not considered lobbying.

Grassroots lobbying is the attempt to influence members of the public to engage in advocacy on specific issues and to encourage members of the organization to urge the public to participate in direct or grassroots lobbying. The activity or communication refers to and reflects a viewpoint on a specific legislative proposal that the organization opposes or supports and it encourages the recipient of the communication to take action.

Whether or not an organizations files under section 501(h), its activity is not lobbying if it entails technical assistance or advice made at the request of the legislature; "self-defense," such as protesting a proposal that would affect the organization's tax exempt status; or nonpartisan research or analysis.

Questions and answers

How does the IRS calculate whether an organization's expenditures are substantial?

For organizations not under section 501(h), there are no set dollar amounts that determine whether lobbying expenses are "substantial." Several criteria are used to determine whether an organization has engaged in substantial lobbying activities, but in general there is no formula. The IRS has wide discretion to find an organization in non-compliance. Sanctions include immediate revocation of the organization's tax-exempt status. For 501(h) electors, there are clear limits and ceilings on lobbying expenses, which are quite generous.

Does the selection of 501(h) compromise the organization's 501(c)(3) status?

No. The 501(c)(3) status relates to exemption from federal tax. The 501(h) determines the method the organization uses for reporting lobbying and grassroots activities.

Can the organization continue to receive foundation grants or federal grants if it chooses the 501(h) election?

Yes. However, as a general rule, federal grant funds should not be used for lobbying purposes. All other private funds of the association can be used for lobbying activities.

What are the advantages of the 501(h) method?

If an organization is audited and has exceeded the allowed amount for lobbying, it will pay taxes only on the excess amount. More important, the organization can maintain its 501(c)(3) status as long as there is not a four-year pattern of exceeding allowed expenditures. Under the substantial compliance test, if the IRS audits the organization and finds that it has exceeded the "substantial" notion, it can immediately repeal the organization's 501(c)(3) status. The 501(h) makes clear the dollar amounts that the organization can commit to lobbying and grassroots activities. The substantial test is generally interpreted as no more than 5% of the organization's tax-exempt budget.

Will the organization more likely be subject to an IRS audit if it elects the 501(h) method?

According to the IRS, the answer is no. The IRS encourages organizations to make the election.

How is the election made?

A simple one-page form is submitted to the IRS. The organization's Governing Board must vote to make the election. Once filed, the 501(h) status applies retroactively for that tax year and applies to subsequent years.

Political activities and voter education

An organization may maintain its federal tax-exempt 501(c)(3) status if it "does not participate in, or intervene in (including the publishing or distributing of statements) any political campaign on behalf of (or in opposition to) any candidate for public office".[2] The sanction for violating these prohibitions is revocation of federal tax-exempt status for a set period of time or permanently. Sometimes a less dramatic sanction is imposed, such as taxing the organization's political expenditures or taxing the organization managers who approved the spending on the political activity. A 501(c)(3) organization with investment income also can be sanctioned with another significant tax on political expenditures.

Questions and answers

Who is a "candidate" for purposes of section 501(c)(3)?

A candidate is anyone who offers himself or herself, or is proposed by others, as a contestant for an elected public office. Organizations under 501(c)(3) cannot urge or draft an individual to declare himself or herself a candidate, organize third-party movements, or do work to explore whether to declare an individual a candidate for elected office.

What is "public office?"

A public office means any position filled by a vote of the people and includes not only the federal elections for president and Congress but also state and local elections, such as school board, city council, and party nominations.

What about candidates for nonpartisan office?

It does not matter. When the Association of the Bar of the City of New York rated judicial candidates on a nonpartisan basis, the IRS revoked the association's 501(c)(3) status.

The Federal Election Campaign Act (FECA), as well as the regulations and rulings of the Federal Election Commission, also set limits for certain kinds of activities. FECA prohibits both for-profit and nonprofit organizations from engaging in campaigns for political candidates. The distinction it makes with respect to allowable activities lies with whether an organization is incorporated or unincorporated and whether it has a membership. Generally speaking, both federal tax law and FECA law and regulations prohibit nonprofit organizations from engaging in political activity that supports a candidate for public office, even nonpartisan office.

Specific activities

Here are some, but not all, specific activities to check against federal election laws and state laws. Below is an explanation relating only to the Internal Revenue Code. Always check for any modifications that may have occurred since your last review.

Endorsement of candidates. The organization, its staff, or members of its board may not support, oppose, or endorse a candidate for public office. Organizations also should avoid using terms like *liberal* or *conservative* or *pro* or *anti*, especially while a political campaign is under way.

Contributions. A 501(c)(3) organization is strictly prohibited from giving any or all candidates a cash or in-kind contribution. The same holds true for contributions to a political action committee (PAC), political party, or fundraising event. Cash contributions include loans. Work on behalf of a candidate is considered an in-kind contribution. Any fundraising sponsorship or solicitation is prohibited. Further, the organization cannot encourage others, including its members, to make contributions.

Membership lists. The organization may rent or sell its membership list to a political group or a candidate only if it (1) charges the full price of the list; (2) offers the list to other candidates or political groups; and (3) reports unrelated business taxable income on the transaction. Giving or lending a membership list to a candidate without payment is an illegal campaign contribution.

Appearance of a candidate at an event. The primary consideration for the IRS is whether the candidate was invited as a candidate or in some other capacity. The IRS looks at other circumstances as well, such as whether political fundraising occurred at the event and whether the other candidates for office were afforded an equal opportunity to participate in the event or a comparable event. The event must not be treated as or become a campaign appearance. The appearance of a candidate, if invited in such capacity, can be seen as an endorsement.

Incumbent office holders. Incumbents—current office holders—create a slightly different set of circumstances. If an organization has lobbied or criticized the actions of an incumbent, then it may continue these activities when the incumbent announces his or her intent to run for re-election. As the election itself nears, however, the IRS may view negative or critical comments about the incumbent as an "intervention" in a political campaign. The IRS will look at whether the organization heightened its level or amount of negative attention, devoted special issues in its materials on an incumbent's record of opposing the organization's position, or distributed an increased number of such materials during the campaign.

Candidate questionnaires. A questionnaire focusing on issues of primary concern to the organization is permissible. However, the way in which the questions are posed must not show any bias or reflect the organization's own agenda. A questionnaire, for example, cannot ask candidates whether they endorse the organization's mission or legislative agenda. Nor can a candidate be asked to sign a pledge. How the responses are disseminated is equally important; candidates' responses must be printed in full exactly as given.

Candidate debates. A 501(c)(3) may sponsor a public debate between candidates if all candidates are invited to participate; an independent panel prepares the questions to be asked; the topics cover a broad set of issues; each candidate has an equal opportunity to express his or her views; and the moderator is neutral and makes a statement both at the beginning and end of the program that the views expressed do not represent those of the sponsoring organization.

Issue briefings. When organizations provide an issue briefing, informing candidates on various issues in person or in writing, the issue briefing must be extended to all candidates running for a particular elected office.

Candidate statements. A 501(c)(3) organization may not distribute candidates' statements to the media, the general public, or to its members until after the election.

Voter guides and vote scorecards. A 501(c)(3) organization is prohibited from using voter guides to support or criticize candidates. Scorecards for how legislators and other officials voted are also a danger zone. An organization can report how legislators vote on issues of concern to the organization, but it must do so regularly, not close to an election or after candidates have declared their intention to run for office.

Testimony on party platforms. Testifying before a platform committee of a political party at the national, state, or local level is permissible lobbying. All parties' platform committees should receive a copy of the testimony. Accounts of the testimony or responses may be reported, but they must be printed in the organization's regularly scheduled publications.

Voter registration and Get Out the Vote (GOTV) drives

A nonprofit organization's work on voter registration and GOTV drives must be nonpartisan. The organization can operate a voter registration table or run a phone bank to encourage the public to go to the polls to vote, but it cannot suggest for whom the public should vote. The organization also must be able to demonstrate that its voter education and registration activities do not help or harm any particular candidate.

Additional resources

The organizations Alliance for Justice, Center for Community Change, and Independent Sector have several publications that can help with the legal ins-and-outs of lobbying, political activities, and voter education (see Appendix E for contact information). Many of their publications are available online for free.

For questions about federal forms, publications, and guidance relating to federal tax laws governing organizations and individuals, contact the Internal Revenue Service. You may contact IRS Customer Service operations concerning tax-exempt organizations at 877-829-5500 (toll-free). The call center is open 8:00AM to 9:30PM Eastern Time. Or you may write: Internal Revenue Service, TE/GE Division, Customer Service, P.O. Box 2508, Cincinnati, OH 45201.

Endnotes

1. Section 501 (c)(3) of the Internal Revenue Code of 1996.
2. *Ibid.*

Children Are Counting on Us

When *Speaking Out: Early Childhood Advocacy* by Goffin and Lombardi was published in 1988, there was great hope that America was on the cusp of some very important commitments to early childhood. Since then, significant changes have indeed occurred: federal funding for child care has expanded, Head Start has flourished, and Early Head Start was created to serve pregnant women and families with infants and toddlers. Most states now offer public kindergarten, and many are beginning to provide prekindergarten services as well. With new research, we now know more about brain development and the relationship between emotional wellness and cognitive development than ever before.

But commitment to early childhood is still woefully inadequate today. Far too many families who qualify for child care assistance do not receive it. In many communities, waiting lists are so long that a child may not even be considered for two or three years. Parents are still the primary financing source for early childhood education. The salaries offered to early childhood program staff are so low that it is next to impossible to attract and retain qualified individuals, especially those who have their own family to raise. Finally, the Family and

Medical Leave Act of 1993 leaves many working parents with the unfair choice of earning a paycheck or spending time with very young or newly adopted children.

America's children need—and certainly deserve—opportunities to reach their fullest potential. This means that they need strong families who can celebrate the wonders of childhood and connect with their children, providing the stable, nurturing, loving environment so important to human development. It also means that children need to have access to high-quality environments that can reinforce the parent-child bond and provide developmentally appropriate experiences when their parents are working or getting an education.

Advocacy efforts—of every type and level—are crucial in effecting positive change for children. It is imperative that parents, grandparents, early care and education providers, teachers, and others involved in the field speak out for children. Whether we are engaged in personal advocacy, public policy advocacy, or private-sector advocacy, it is important that all of us who touch the lives of children do all we can to educate the American public about the needs of children and the social and moral responsibility of our society to care for children. Our children's cries will continue to go unheard unless we stand up for them. Children can't do it themselves—they are counting on us.

APPENDICES

The Structure of the Federal Government and the Role of the Legislative Branch

The U.S. Constitution sets up three branches of federal power: the Executive Branch, the Legislative Branch, and the Judicial Branch. Article II of the Constitution places executive power in the president, who serves a four-year term and is limited to two elected terms. Article I of the Constitution states that "all legislative Powers herein granted shall be vested in a Congress of the United States, which shall consist of a Senate and House of Representatives."

A Congress sits for a two-year period. For example, the 107th Congress was sworn into office on January 3, 2001. The first session ends in the fall of 2001. The second session commences in January 2002, and the 107th Congress formally ends when the Congress goes *sine die* (adjourns on the final day of the session).

The Senate consists of 100 elected members, two from each state. The term of office is six years and there is no limit on the number of terms a senator can serve. The terms are staggered so that every two years one-third of the Senate is up for re-election. The staggered terms ensure that both senators from a single state do not end their terms in the same year. The senator who has served longer in the Senate is known as the "senior senator."

The House of Representatives consists of 435 elected members, each representing a Congressional district of approximately 600,000 people. The number of representatives reflects a state's population as reported in the decennial census. When redistricting occurs in a state due to population shifts, the number of seats may change. Representatives serve for two-year terms. Unlike in the Senate, all Representatives are up for re-election at the same time.

The House and the Senate have similar legislative functions with the following exceptions: Any bill that requires the raising (tax bills) or spending (appropriations bills) of federal dollars must originate with the House. Any political appointment or Supreme Court appointment requires confirmation by the U.S. Senate.

Both the House and Senate are organized with committees for specific areas of lawmaking (such as education, taxes, appropriations, agriculture) and with leadership offices. The members of the House of Representatives elect a Speaker of the House from the majority party and the party in the minority (those with fewer members) elects a minority leader. The leaders in the Senate are the Majority leader and Minority leader.

Legislative Staff

These terms are typically used for staff working for members of Congress, but your state legislators may use similar staff titles. Some of these titles are used for staff on committees, such as "legislative assistant."

Chief of staff—This person often has an integral part of the legislator's campaign team and is relied upon for his or her sense of the politics of the legislator's district or state.

Legislative director—The "LD" oversees all of the staff handling legislation.

Legislative assistant—There are several legislative assistants in each office and on each committee. Each handles a set of issues. They follow a bill from beginning to end, meet with advocacy groups concerned with the legislation, and make recommendations to the legislator on how to act on the bill as it moves through the process.

Press secretary/communications director—The press secretary works with the media, answering their questions and issuing press releases.

Appointment secretary—This person schedules visits with the member of Congress. Most offices require a fax or letter requesting a meeting; a phone call will not suffice.

State Government

State government has many similarities with federal government, but each state has a unique constitution (although all of them must abide by the U.S. Constitution), its own rules and procedures, its terminology, and its political history and culture.

Governor and Lieutenant Governor

The governor is the state's chief executive officer. His or her powers vary greatly from state to state. Most have a term of office of four years; governors have two-year terms in New Hampshire and Vermont. Most governors are term-limited. Their responsibilities and powers cover the general administration of state government, including making appointments to state agencies and commissions; preparing and submitting the proposed budget; signing or vetoing legislation; and exercising the line-item veto (although not all states grant line-item veto power). The election cycle usually coincides with federal elections (exceptions are New Jersey and Virginia, which elect governors in "off" election years).

The governor is usually the most powerful policy leader in the state. The power flows from the authority granted constitutionally, the political leadership that may be exercised, and the "bully-pulpit" influence of this prestigious position.

The lieutenant governor may be elected on a slate with the governor or separately. In states where they are elected separately, occasionally the governor and lieutenant governor are not members of the same political party. As a general rule, however, the lieutenant governor is a stalwart supporter of the governor, fulfilling assignments made by the governor and ready to step into the top position should a vacancy occur for any reason. Most lieutenant governors preside over the state Senates. In some states, such as Texas, the lieutenant governor is in charge of formulating the state's budget.

State legislatures

Every state has a legislature and, in every state except Nebraska, it is bicameral (consisting of two bodies). States refer to the upper house as the Senate, but may call the lower body the General Assembly, House of Representatives, or House of Delegates. The Republican and Democratic members of the House and Senate typically elect their caucus leaders, who serve as majority or minority leader in their respective chambers. Each party caucus usually elects additional members to other policy or administrative posts. The presiding officer in the Senate is usually the lieutenant governor or the president *pro tem* (for the time being). The presiding officer in the lower body is the speaker.

The political culture varies greatly among the states. In some instances, committee chairs are very powerful, and in other states most power resides in a handful of leadership positions. Often the power of personality is as important as the authority of a particular position. The dynamics of relationships can be as significant as the structure and rules of the legislature in determining how legislation is considered and to what end.

State senators usually serve four-year terms and members in the lower body serve for two years. Unlike in the U.S. Congress, there are term limits for many state legislators. The majority of legislatures are not full-year bodies. In some states the legislature meets only every other year or has only a limited agenda in the "off" year.

Excerpt from Section 501(c)(3) of the Internal Revenue Code

Sec. 501. Exemption from tax on corporations, certain trusts, etc.

(a) Exemption from taxation

An organization described in subsection (c) or (d) or section 401(a) shall be exempt from taxation under this subtitle unless such exemption is denied under section 502 or 503.

(b) Tax on unrelated business income and certain other activities

An organization exempt from taxation under subsection (a) shall be subject to tax to the extent provided in parts II, III, and VI of this subchapter, but (notwithstanding parts II, III, and VI of this subchapter) shall be considered an organization exempt from income taxes for the purpose of any law which refers to organizations exempt from income taxes.

(c) List of exempt organizations

The following organizations are referred to in subsection (a):

. . .

(3) Corporations, and any community chest, fund, or foundation, organized and operated exclusively for religious, charitable, scientific, testing for public safety, literary, or educational purposes, or to foster national or international amateur sports competition (but only if no part of its activities involve the provision of athletic facilities or equipment), or for the prevention of cruelty to children or animals, no part of the net earnings of which inures to the benefit of any private shareholder or individual, no substantial part of the activities of which is carrying on propaganda, or otherwise attempting, to influence legislation (except as otherwise provided in subsection (h)), and which does not participate in, or intervene in (including the publishing or distributing of statements), any political campaign on behalf of (or in opposition to) any candidate for public office.

Organizational Resources for Early Childhood Advocates

Federal Government

U.S. Department of Commerce
  Bureau of the Census
Washington, DC 20233
Public Information Office: 301-763-7662
Data User Services Division: 301-763-4100
General telephone inquiries: 301-457-4608
www.census.gov

U.S. Department of Education
400 Maryland Avenue, SW
Washington, DC 20202-0498
Phone: 1-800-USA-LEARN
    (1-800-872-5327)
www.ed.gov

U.S. Department of Health and
  Human Services
Administration of Children, Youth
  and Families
Child Care Bureau
Switzer Building, Room 2046
330 C Street, SW
Washington, DC 20447
Phone: 202-690-6782
www.acf.dhhs.gov/programs/ccb

U.S. Department of Health and
  Human Services
Administration of Children, Youth
  and Families
Head Start Bureau
330 C Street, SW
Washington, DC 20447
Phone: 202-205-8572
www2.acf.dhhs.gov/programs/hsb

U.S. Department of Labor
  Bureau of Labor Statistics
Postal Square Building
2 Massachusetts Avenue, NE
Washington, DC 20212-0001
Phone: 202-691-5200
http://stats.bls.gov

U.S. Department of Labor
  Office of Public Affairs
200 Constitution Avenue, NW
Room S-1032
Washington, DC 20210
Phone: 202-693-4650
www.dol.gov

State Government

National Conference of State
  Legislatures
Denver Office:
1560 Broadway, Suite 700
Denver, CO 80202
Phone: 303-830-2200

Washington, DC Office:
444 North Capitol Street, NW
Suite 515
Washington, DC 20001
Phone: 202-624-5400
www.ncsl.org

National Governors' Association
  Hall of States
444 North Capitol Street, NW
Washington, DC 20001-1512
Phone: 202-624-5300
www.nga.org

Organizations

Alliance for Early Childhood Finance
www.earlychildhoodfinance.org

Alliance for Justice
11 Dupont Circle, NW
Suite 200
Washington, DC 20036
Phone: 202-822-6070
www.allianceforjustice.org

American Academy of Pediatrics
Headquarters:
141 Northwest Point Boulevard
Elk Grove Village, IL 60007-1098
Phone: 847-434-4000

Washington, DC Office:
Department of Federal Affairs
601 13th Street, NW
Suite 400 North
Washington, DC 20005
Phone: 202-347-8600
www.aap.org

**American Association of Colleges for
Teacher Education**
1307 New York Avenue, NW, Suite 300
Washington, DC 20005-4701
Phone: 202-293-2450
www.aacte.org

**American Association of University
Women**
1111 16th Street, NW
Washington, DC 20036
Phone: 202-785-7715
Toll Free: 800-326-2289
www.aauw.org

**American Bar Association
The National Legal Resource
Center for Child Advocacy and
Protection**
1800 M Street, NW, Suite 200 South
Washington, DC 20036
Phone: 202-331-2250

American Federation of Teachers
555 New Jersey Avenue, NW
Washington, DC 20001
Phone: 202-879-4400
www.aft.org

**American Federation of State, County
and Municipal Employees**
1625 L Street, NW
Washington, DC 20036
Phone: 202-429-1000
www.afcme.org

American Psychological Association
750 First Street, NE
Washington, DC 20002-4242
Phone: 202-336-5510
Toll Free: 800-374-2721
www.apa.org

Center for Community Change
Washington, DC Office:
1000 Wisconsin Avenue, NW
Washington, DC 20007
Phone: 202-342-0567

San Francisco Office:
160 Sansome Street, 7th Floor
San Francisco, CA 94104
Phone: 415-982-0346
www.communitychange.org

**The Center for the Child Care
Workforce**
733 15th Street, NW, Suite 1037
Washington, DC 20005-2112
Phone: 202-737-7700
Toll Free: 800-U-R-Worthy
www.ccw.org

Center on Budget and Policy Priorities
820 First Street, NE, #510
Washington, DC 20002
Phone: 202-408-1080
www.cbpp.org

Center for Law and Social Policy
1015 15th Street, NW, Suite 400
Washington, DC 20005
Phone: 202-906-8000
www.clasp.org

Child Care Action Campaign
330 Seventh Avenue, 14th Floor,
New York, NY 10001
Phone: 212-239-0138
www.childcareaction.org

Child Care Law Center
973 Market Street, Suite 550
San Francisco, CA 94103
Phone: 415-495-5498
www.childcarelaw.org

Child Trends
4301 Connecticut Avenue, NW
Suite 100
Washington, DC 20008
Phone: 202-362-5580
www.childtrends.org

Child Welfare League of America
Headquarters:
440 First Street, NW, Third Floor
Washington, DC 20001-2085
Program Office:
50 F Street NW, 6th Floor
Washington, DC 20001-2085
Phone: 202-638-2952
www.cwla.org

Children's Defense Fund
25 E Street, NW
Washington, DC 20001
Phone: 202-628-8787
www.childrensdefense.org

Committee for Economic Development
New York Office:
477 Madison Avenue
New York, NY 10022
Phone: 212-688-2063

Washington, DC Office:
2000 L Street, NW, Suite 700
Washington, DC 20036
Phone: 202-296-5860
www.ced.org

Concerned Educators Allied for a Safe Environment (CEASE)
17 Gerry Street
Cambridge, MA 02138
Phone: 617-864-0999

Council for Exceptional Children
1110 North Glebe Road, Suite 300
Arlington, VA 22201-5704
Phone: 703-620-3660
Toll Free: 888-CEC-SPED
www.cec.sped.org

Council for Professional Recognition
2460 16th Street, NW
Washington, DC 20009-3575
Phone: 202-265-9090
Toll Free: 800-424-4310
www.cdacouncil.org

Council of Chief State School Officers
One Massachusetts Avenue, NW
Suite 700
Washington, DC 20001-1431
Phone: 202-408-5505
www.ccsso.org

Division for Early Childhood of the Council for Exceptional Children
1380 Lawrence Street, Suite 650
Denver, CO 80204
Phone: 303-556-3328
www.dec-sped.org

Ecumenical Child Care Network
8765 West Higgins Road, Suite 405
Chicago, IL 60631
Phone: 773-696-4040
Toll Free: 800-694-5443
www.eccn.org

Education Commission of the States
707 17th Street, #2700
Denver, CO 80202-3427
Phone: 303-299-3600
www.ecs.org

ERIC Clearinghouse on Elementary and
  Early Childhood Education (ERIC/PS)
University of Illinois at Urbana-
  Champaign
Children's Research Center
51 Gerty Drive
Champaign, IL 61820-7469
Phone: 217-333-1386
Toll Free: 800-583-4135
http://ericeece.org

Families and Work Institute
330 Seventh Avenue, 14th Floor
New York, NY 10001
Phone: 212-465-2044
www.familiesandwork.org

Food Research and Action Center
1875 Connecticut Avenue, NW
Suite 540
Washington, DC 20009
Phone: 202-986-2200
www.frac.org

Foundation for Child Development
145 East 32nd Street, 14th Floor
New York, NY 10016-6055
Phone: 212-213-8337
www.ffcd.org

Generations United
122 C Street, NW, Suite 820
Washington, DC 20001
Phone: 202-638-1263
www.gu.org

High/Scope Educational Research
  Foundation
600 North River Street
Ypsilanti, MI 48198-2898

Phone: 734-485-2000
www.highscope.org

I Am Your Child
Beverly Hills Office:
PO Box 15605
Beverly Hills, CA 90209
Phone: 310-285-2385

New York Office:
1325 6th Avenue, 30th Floor
New York, NY 10019
Phone: 212-636-5030
www.iamyourchild.org

Independent Sector
1200 18th Street, NW
Suite 200
Washington, DC 20036
Phone: 202-467-6100
www.independentsector.org

Initiative & Referendum Institute
1825 I Street, NW, Suite 400
Washington, DC 20006
Phone: 202-429-5539
www.iandrinstitute.org

International Reading Association
Headquarters:
800 Barksdale Road
PO Box 8139
Newark, DE 19714-8139
Phone: 302-731-1600

Washington, DC Office:
444 North Capitol Street, NW
Suite 630
Washington, DC 20001
Phone: 202-624-8800
www.ira.org

Kiwanis International
3636 Woodview Trace
Indianapolis, IN 46268-3196
Phone: 317-875-8755
www.kiwanis.org

National Association for Bilingual Education
1030 15th Street, NW, Suite 470
Washington, DC 20005
Phone: 202-898-1829
www.nabe.org

National Association for Family Child Care
5202 Pinemont Drive
Salt Lake City, UT 84123
Phone: 801-269-9338
Toll Free: 800-359-3817
www.nafcc.org

National Association for Regulatory Administration
Eastern Office:
905 Schoolhouse Lane
Dover, DE 19904
Phone: 302-678-4775

Western Office:
26 East Exchange Street, Fifth Floor
St. Paul, MN 55101-2264
Phone: 651-290-6280
www.nara-licensing.org

National Association of Child Care Resource and Referral Agencies
1319 F Street, NW, Suite 500
Washington, DC 20004-1106
Phone: 202-393-5501
www.naccrra.org

National Association of Early Childhood Specialists in State Departments of Education
http://ericps.crc.uiuc.edu/naecs

National Association of Early Childhood Teacher Educators
www.naecte.org

The National Association of Elementary School Principals
1615 Duke Street
Alexandria, VA 22314
Phone: 703-684-3345
Toll Free: 800-386-2377
www.naesp.org

National Association of Social Workers
750 First Street, NE, Suite 700
Washington, DC 20002-4241
Phone: 202-408-8600
Toll Free: 800-638-8799
www.naswdc.org

National Association of State Boards of Education
277 South Washington Street, Suite 100
Alexandria, VA 22314
Phone: 703-684-4000
www.nasbe.org

National Association of State Directors of Special Education
1800 Diagonal Road, Suite 320
Alexandria, VA 22314
Phone: 703-519-3800
www.nasdse.org

National Black Child Development Institute
1101 15th Street NW, Suite 900
Washington, DC 20005
Phone: 202-833-2220
www.nbcdi.org

National Center for Children in Poverty
The Joseph L. Mailman School of Public Health of Columbia University
154 Haven Avenue
New York, NY 10032
Phone: 212-304-7100
http://cpmcnet.columbia.edu/dept/nccp

National Child Care Association
1016 Rosser Street
Conyers, GA 30012
Toll Free: 800-543-7161
www.nccanet.org

**National Child Care Information
  Center**
243 Church Street, NW
2nd Floor
Vienna, VA 22180
Phone: 800-616-2242
http://nccic.org

**National Clearinghouse for Military
  Child Development Program**
Military Family Resource Center
CS4, Suite 302, Room 309
1745 Jefferson Davis Highway
Arlington, VA 22202-3424
Phone: 703-602-4964
Toll Free: 888-CDP-3040
http://military-childrenandyouth.calib.com

**National Coalition for Campus
  Children's Centers**
119 Schindler Education Center
University of Northern Iowa
Cedar Falls, IA 50614
Phone: 319-273-3113
Toll Free: 800-813-8207
www.campuschildren.org

**National Council for Accreditation of
  Teacher Education**
2010 Massachusetts Avenue, NW
Suite 500
Washington, DC 20036-1023
Phone: 202-466-7496
www.ncate.org

National Council of Jewish Women
New York Office:
53 West 23rd Street, 6th Floor
New York, NY 10010-4204
Phone: 212-645-4048

Washington, DC Office:
1707 L Street, NW, Suite 950
Washington, DC 20036
Phone: 202-296-9588
www.ncjw.org

National Council of La Raza
1111 19th Street, NW
Suite 1000
Washington, DC 20036
Phone: 202-785-1670
www.nclr.org

**The National Council of Negro
  Women, Inc.**
633 Pennsylvania Avenue, NW
Washington, DC 20004
Phone: 202-737-0120
www.ncnw.com

National Education Association
1201 16th Street, NW
Washington, DC 20036
Phone: 202-833-4000
www.nea.org

National Head Start Association
1651 Prince Street
Alexandria, VA 22314
Phone: 703-739-0875
www.nhsa.org

**National Institute on Early Childhood
  Development and Education**
Office of Educational Research
  and Improvement
U.S. Department of Education
555 New Jersey Avenue, NW
Washington, DC 20208
Phone: 202-219-1935
www.ed.gov/offices/OERI/ECI

National Institute on Out-of-School Time
Wellesley College
106 Central Street
Wellesley, MA 02481
Phone: 781-283-2547
www.noist.org

National Latino Children's Institute
320 El Paso Street
San Antonio, TX 78207
Phone: 210-228-9997 or
512-472-9971 (Austin)
www.nlci.org

National League of Cities
1301 Pennsylvania Avenue, NW
Suite 550
Washington, DC 20004
Phone: 202-626-3000
www.nlc.org

National Organization for Women (NOW) Legal Defense and Education Fund
New York Office;
395 Hudson Street
New York, NY 10014
Phone: 212-925-6635

Washington, DC Office:
1522 K Street, NW
Suite 550
Washington, DC 20005
Phone: 202-326-0040
www.nowldef.org

National PTA
330 North Wabash Avenue
Suite 2100
Chicago, IL 60611
Phone: 312-670-6782
Toll Free: 800-307-4782
www.pta.org

National School Boards Association
1680 Duke Street
Alexandria, VA 22314-3493
Phone: 703-838-6722
www.nsba.org

National Women's Law Center
11 Dupont Circle, NW
Suite 800
Washington, DC 20036
Phone: 202-588-5180
www.nwlc.org

PBS—Ready to Learn
1320 Braddock Place
Alexandria, VA 22314
Phone: 703-739-5000
http://pbskids.org/grownups/
readytolearn.html

Society for Research in Child Development
University of Michigan
505 East Huron
Suite 301
Ann Arbor, MI 48104-1567
Phone: 734-998-6578
www.srcd.org

Southern Early Childhood Association
PO Box 55930
Little Rock, AR 72215-5930
Phone: 800-305-7322
www.seca50.org

Stand for Children
1420 Columbia Road, NW
3rd Floor
Washington, DC 20009
Phone: 202-234-0095
Toll Free: 800-663-4032
www.stand.org

United Way of America
701 North Fairfax Street
Alexandria, VA 22314-2045
Phone: 703-836-7100
www.unitedway.org

The Urban Institute
2100 M Street, NW
Washington, DC 20037
Phone: 202-833-7200
www.urban.org

USA Child Care
243 Church Street, NW, 2nd Floor
Vienna, VA 22180
Phone: 703-938-5531
www.usachildcare.org

**Wheelock College Institute for
  Leadership and Career Initiatives
(formerly Center for Career Development in Early Care and Education)**
Wheelock College
200 The Riverway
Boston, MA 02215-4176

Phone: 617-879-2211
http://institute.wheelock.edu

**Young Men's Christian Association
  of the USA**
101 North Wacker Drive
Chicago, IL 60606
Phone: 312-977-0031
www.ymca.net

**Young Women's Christian Association
  of the USA**
Empire State Building
350 Fifth Avenue, Suite 301
New York, NY 10118
Phone: 212-273-7800
www.ywca.org

**ZERO TO THREE: National Center
  for Infants, Toddlers and Families**
2000 M Street, NW
Suite 200
Washington, DC 20036
Phone: 202-638-1144
www.zerotothree.org

Please see our webpage at **www.naeyc.org** for the most current
NAEYC Affiliate contact information.

Information about NAEYC

NAEYC is . . .

an organization of nearly 100,000 members, founded in 1926, that is committed to fostering the development and learning of children from birth through age 8. Membership is open to all who share a commitment to promote excellence in early childhood education and to act on behalf of the needs and rights of all children.

NAEYC provides . . .

• *Young Children,* the peer-reviewed journal for early childhood educators

• **Books, posters, brochures, and videos** to expand your knowledge and commitment and support your work with young children and families

• **A network of nearly 450 local, state, and regional Affiliates**

• **Research-based position statements and professional standards** on issues such as inclusion, diversity, literacy, assessment, developmentally appropriate practice, and teacher preparation

• **Professional development resources and programs,** including the annual National Institute for Early Childhood Professional Development, improving the quality and consistency of early childhood professional preparation and leadership

• **Public policy information** through NAEYC resources and the Children's Champions Action Center, for conducting effective advocacy in government and in the media

• **An Annual Conference,** the largest education conference in North America, that brings people together from across the United States and other countries to share their expertise and advocate on behalf of children and families

• **A national, voluntary, professionally sponsored accreditation system** for high-quality early education through the National Academy of Early Childhood Programs

• *Early Childhood Research Quarterly,* the field's leading scholarly publication; special rate for NAEYC members

• **Young Children International,** encouraging information exchange and networking among NAEYC's international colleagues

• **Week of the Young Child** celebrations planned annually by NAEYC Affiliate Groups in communities across the country to call public attention to the critical significance of the child's early years

• **Insurance plans** for members and programs

For information about membership, publications, or other NAEYC services, visit NAEYC online at www.naeyc.org.

**National Association for the Education of Young Children
1509 16th Street, NW
Washington, DC 20036-1426
202-232-8777 or 800-424-2460**